A
Therapeutic
Library

Published in 2023 by The School of Life
First published in the USA in 2023
930 High Road, London, N12 9RT

Copyright © The School of Life 2023

Designed and typeset by Marcia Mihotich
Printed in Latvia by Livonia Print

A proportion of this book has appeared online at
www.theschooloflife.com/articles

Every effort has been made to contact the
copyright holders of the material reproduced
in this book. If any have been inadvertently
overlooked, the publisher will be pleased to
make restitution at the earliest opportunity.

The School of Life publishes a range of books on
essential topics in psychological and emotional
life, including relationships, parenting,
friendship, careers and fulfilment. The aim is
always to help us to understand ourselves better
and thereby to grow calmer, less confused and
more purposeful. Discover our full range of
titles, including books for children, here:
www.theschooloflife.com/books

The School of Life also offers a
comprehensive therapy service, which
complements, and draws upon, our published
works: www.theschooloflife.com/therapy

ISBN 978-1-915087-38-6

10 9 8 7 6 5 4 3 2 1

A
Therapeutic
Library

The School of Life

Introduction

Introduction:
On Therapeutic Reading

On average, a person might read 1,000 books in their lifetime. If they are doing especially well, it might be 2,000 or 3,000. The issue is that there are around 130 million books in the world, and they are being added to at a rate of 4 or so million a year.

In other words, from the perspective of numbers alone, the onus is on us to choose very carefully indeed.

One of the challenges in doing so is that most of the noise around books concerns the newest titles. Many of these are worthy, but by definition they represent only the latest output in the long history of writing. It is therefore unlikely that, of all the books we could choose from, the ones most useful to us will be among those released in the preceding twelve months.

Another challenge lies in the distribution of prestige. Our societies tend to operate with powerful lists of books they deem hugely significant. It is to these that our attention is drawn from an early age and that seem to hold the key to enlightenment and wisdom. Many of these books are indeed astonishing and brilliant, but a great many more might, if we could dare to say what we really thought, strike us as turgid and irrelevant.

Honesty then becomes a central problem. The fear of disliking or being bored by a book deemed a masterpiece by prestigious voices holds us back from being properly ourselves. We stymie our authentic interests and risk in time losing a personal connection with books altogether. We need works that will change *our* lives and have a revelatory influence on *our* minds, not books that had a momentous impact on *other* people who were probably quite unlike us. Fame alone can't be the guide to a true relationship with a work of literature.

While resisting the pressure to make our way through an ever-larger number of titles, we might pause to reflect on a fascinating aspect of the premodern world: this world rarely put people under any pressure to read very much at all. Reading was held to be extremely important, but the number of new books one read was entirely by the by. This wasn't principally an economic point. Books were very expensive, of course, but this wasn't really the issue. What mattered was to read a few books very well, not to squander one's attention promiscuously on a great number of volumes.

The premodern world directed people to read so little because it was obsessed by a question that modernity likes to dodge: *what is the point of reading?* And it had answers. To take a supreme example, Christians and Muslims located the value of reading in a very specific and narrow goal: the attainment of holiness. To read was to try to approximate the mind of God. In each case this meant that one book, and one book only – the Bible or the Quran – was held up as vastly and incomparably more important than any other. To read this book, repeatedly and with great attention, probably five or so pages every day, was thought more crucial than to rush through a whole library every week. In fact, reading widely would have been regarded with suspicion, because most other books would to some extent have to prove misleading and distracting.

Similarly, in the Ancient Greek world, one was meant to focus in on a close knowledge of just two books, Homer's *Odyssey* and *Iliad*, because these were deemed the perfect repository of the Greek code of honour and the best guides to action in military and civilian affairs.

We can pick up some of this minimalist attitude to reading in early visual depictions of one of the heroes of Christian scholarship, Saint Jerome. He was considered one of the supreme intellects of Christendom, a man who translated the Greek and Hebrew portions of the Bible into Latin, wrote a large number of commentaries on scripture and became the patron saint of libraries and librarians.

But despite all his scholarly efforts, when it came to depictions of Saint Jerome, one detail stands out: there are almost no books in his famous study. Strikingly, the most intelligent and thoughtful intellectual of the early church seems to have read fewer things than an average modern 8-year-old. In this painting by Antonello da Messina, Saint Jerome appears to be the proud owner of no more than around ten books.

Antonello da Messina,
Saint Jerome in his Study, c. 1475

The modern world has dramatically parted ways with this minimalist ancient approach to reading. We have adopted an Enlightenment viewpoint that runs in a very different direction, stating that there should be no limit to how much we read. In considering why we do so, there is only one response that will ever be encompassing or ambitious enough: *we read in order to know everything*.

However, we can hazard an observation: this exhaustive approach to reading does not make us particularly happy. In order to ease and simplify our lives, we might dare to ask a very old-fashioned question: *what am I reading for?* This time, rather than answering 'in order to know everything', we might have a much more limited, focused and useful goal. We might decide on a new mantra to guide our reading henceforth: *we want to read in order to learn to be content*.

With this new, more targeted, ambition in mind, much of the pressure to read constantly and randomly starts to fade. Once we know that we are reading to be content, we don't need to chase every book published this season. We can zero in on titles that best explain what we deem to be the constituent parts of contentment. For example, we may need a few key books that will explain our psyches to us, that will teach us about how families work and how they might work better, that can take us through how to find a job we can love or how to develop the courage to develop our opportunities. We'll probably need some books that talk about friendship and love, sexuality and health, and some that gently guide us to how to minimise regret and learn to die well.

This is why we have written this book: it amounts to a list of the books that might be key in helping us to lead less agitated, dispirited or pained lives; it is a guide to an ideal therapeutic library.

The more we understand what reading is for us, the more we can enjoy intimate relationships with a few works only. The truly well-read person isn't one who has read a gargantuan number of books; it is someone who has let themselves be deeply shaped by just a few well-chosen titles.

Raphael, *School of Athens*, Aristotle and
Plato at the centre, c. 1509–1511

*The purpose of literature is to
treat disorders of the mind, just as
the purpose of medicine is to treat
disorders of the body.*

Aristotle,
Poetics, c. 335 BCE

Far from being a new or marginal approach, the idea of books as therapy goes back to the earliest Western ideas about what reading is for. The *Poetics*, written by Aristotle around 335 BCE, when he was in his 50s and living in Athens, focuses on one major strand of literature: tragic stories in which terrible things happen to decent people. Such stories were traditionally presented on stage at public festivals all over Ancient Greece, but the texts were also readily available. Aristotle asks a fundamental question: what's the point of engaging with such tales? Aren't there enough horrors in the world?

His answer is this: a well-told tragedy explains the small, understandable steps, such as anyone might make in the circumstances, that lead 'a slightly better than average person', as we may take ourselves to be, with ordinary, minor flaws of character, to ruin and disgrace. The art of the tragic writer is to provide a compelling explanation of how and why such a terrible fate could befall us or people we love. Tragedy moves us to pity and compassion because it makes us feel close to the troubles that we'd prefer to feel could only happen to distant others.

In Aristotle's eyes, tragedy is a cure – or therapy – for a specific problem of the psyche or soul: indifference or hardness of heart. Specifically, he calls the cure a 'catharsis' or unblocking. Our instinctive sympathy for others, which we felt as children, gets stopped by our adult preoccupation with success; the right stories help tenderness flow again.

Up to this point, 'therapy' had mainly been used in connection with medicine, where it meant any treatment of a bodily disorder. Aristotle, who had trained as a doctor and came from a successful medical family, simply extends the idea of treatment to what he called the *psyche*, meaning the mind or the soul. The notion of psychotherapy has one of its taproots here, in this unexpected place: in Aristotle's discussion of why we should read certain kinds of stories.

Aristotle's approach has a particular structure. Like a medical doctor, he diagnoses a problem (the blockage of sympathy) and then recommends a specific therapy (well-written tragic drama). This is the approach we're going to follow too. The reason for recommending a work isn't that it is broadly 'interesting' or 'something every well-educated person should have read' but more private and psychological. The book can be seen as offering a 'cure' or at least a helpful treatment for a particular suffering or sorrow of inner life.

We're not suggesting that all the books discussed in this book are for everyone. Rather, we are exploring the therapeutic help that certain works offer. But which kinds of therapy any of us need depends on the specifics of our own minds: the spendthrift needs different book friends from the miser; the overly shy person needs different recommendations than the person who cannot bear to be alone with themselves. We are in search of the books that can cure our particular ailments.

Alexandre-Hyacinthe Dunouy, *Jean-Jacques Rousseau dans le parc de Rochecardon*, 1795

Because we are reading for therapy – the healing of our souls – we can take a seemingly unconventional approach to engaging with a book.

Jean-Jacques Rousseau, *Reveries of a Solitary Walker*, 1782

Typically, we imagine that we're supposed to read the whole book in the proper sequence, from page one through to the end.

Born in Geneva in 1712, the son of an industrious but not especially successful watchmaker, in his teens Jean-Jacques Rousseau ran away from his native city and began a life of wandering, mainly in France. He worked for a time as a footman, but in his 30s became celebrated first as a composer of music, then as a writer. He much preferred solitude to elegant society; he was an awkward, intense individual and quarrelled, eventually, with all those who tried to befriend him.

In old age he wrote a sequence of meditations that he called *reveries*, describing the seemingly random thoughts that came to him on his long, solitary strolls around the outskirts of Paris. The title is beguiling, because we all have our own reveries: our private musings on what happened yesterday or five years ago or something we heard someone say. We spin off in unexpected directions, we ask ourselves questions we can't answer or think of the perfect solution to a problem we had a decade ago.

As we read, we come across little phrases that touch off our own trains of thought. Near the start of the third chapter, Rousseau says: 'I'm saddened by what experience has taught me; ignorance would be preferable.' We stop wanting to hear about him and want to use this phrase to examine our own lives. What, in fact, has experience taught *us*? Has it helped us? Would it be better never to have learned certain hard lessons? We might never read the rest of the chapter, but that's fine: we've met an idea that becomes a personal question. If we were sitting an exam, this would be a disaster: we've no idea what precisely he had in mind. But in therapeutic reading our goal isn't to understand Rousseau but to understand ourselves.

Later we're flicking idly through the pages and hit on a passage in chapter five. It's rather lovely: he's remembering when he lived alone on a small island in a Swiss lake. We might stop reading here. Where, in fantasy, would we like to live? Why does the picture of a wooded island appeal so much? But we press on for a few more paragraphs and find Rousseau lying in a little boat being rocked by the gentle waves and asking himself: 'Who am I really, in and of myself?' Theoretically, we're supposed to be eager to hear *his* answer. But as therapeutic readers we feel the question as our own. We don't bother to read on. He's set up the relaxed atmosphere and then fired a question into the heart of who we are. Perhaps we'll never read another word of the book.

Can we say we've read the *Reveries*? By the banal standard of a book review, of course not: we've absorbed only a couple of paragraphs. But we've got what we needed. This might be one of the most important books we ever come across.

Maurice Jarnoux, *André Malraux with his
imaginary library of images at his house
in Boulogne-sur-Seine near Paris*, 1953

*We want to surround ourselves with the
images – and books and people – who
speak deeply and wisely to our souls.*

André Malraux,
The Voices of Silence, 1951

Around the middle of the 20th century, the relationship between individuals and art underwent a dramatic change. Up to that point, in order to see a famous work, one had to visit it *in situ*, in a great gallery, a church or a temple, or buy an expensive copy. By the late 1940s, however, the costs of photographic reproduction and printing had fallen sufficiently that large numbers of people could, for the first time, see what works of art from across the world, and from all times, looked like.

The writer who had the most interesting response to this was the French novelist, philosopher, archaeologist and politician André Malraux. He realised that from then on the problem would never be how we could have access to art – in fact, we'd be inundated with images. Instead, the urgent task was to work out what we wanted to do with this new opportunity.

In *Les Voix du Silence* (*The Voices of Silence*), published in France in 1951, Malraux argues that our task is to create 'an imaginary museum' of our own: a personal selection from the art of the world that draws together the objects that have 'the power to help us live'. He himself was drawn to images of the human face in moments of intense thought or contemplation, coming from ancient China, medieval Nigeria, Mexico and from Maori artists.

In a comparable spirit, we are building an imaginary library of books. Ironically, it's another, more recent, technological change that has altered, and perhaps deepened, our relationship to books. While so much else has been transformed, books, as physical objects, remain stubbornly offline. They're not smart or connected: they don't keep up with the news; they're indifferent to fashion; they're slow, quiet and long term.

The books we love treat us with great dignity: they want us to be thoughtful, serious, sensitive and emotionally complex. They're not in a hurry: they want us to linger, consider, digest and reflect. The books that matter to us can't go out of date. They are past craving popularity. It makes no difference to them if they are read by millions or only by us. They don't mind if it's a few years before we get round to reading them or if we simply glance at them from time to time or if we put them down for a while. They invite us into a world of sanity.

As with people, we'll only properly make friends with a limited number of books across our lives. In our imaginary library, we're bringing these friends together; they interact, converse and have interesting arguments in our minds.

Touchingly, Malraux suggested that we are doing an essential service to the art we admire when we include it in our collection. Big public museums and libraries are, he thought, where things go to die. They are famous, perhaps, but they're not communicating intimately. We all need to build up a library that precisely matches our longings, confusions and hopes.

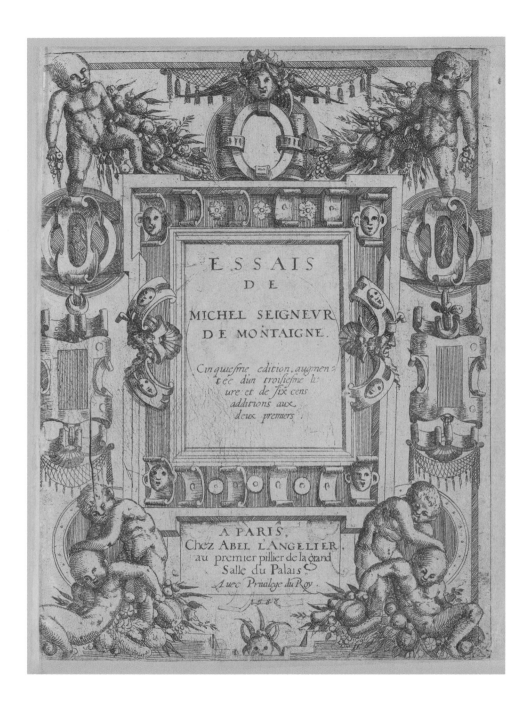

Michel de Montaigne, *Essais (Essays)*,
frontispiece of edition published in 1588

A deeply personal exploration of the
strangeness and fascination of the
human condition — one that offers help
in many different directions.

Michel de Montaigne, *Essays,* 1580

It might be possible to list books according to the particular need they address. We could perhaps group together all the works that offer friendship and keep them apart from those that offer perspective or those that remind us of simple, but always vanishing, truths. However, there are many books that are difficult to categorise because, within a single set of covers, they are potentially therapeutic in multiple ways. One such work is the collection of essays written across many years by the 16th-century French philosopher, lawyer, diplomat and (at times) recluse, Michel de Montaigne.

At one point, Montaigne might remind us of something we instinctively know but don't keep at the front of our minds: 'On the highest throne in the world, we are seated still upon our arses'; however potent an individual seems, they really are human. In the abstract, of course, we ascribe to this. But when we're in the company of highly successful people, the insight tends to evaporate: we become deferential and timid. He's not suggesting we become defiant or mocking; the real goal is authentic connection – Montaigne himself was a close friend of the King of France. What he means is that remembering that someone is human helps us get on with them. The therapeutic move concerns our stultifying sense of distance: if we treat the grand other as the imperfect, ordinary being they really are, they will (quite possibly) respond warmly.

At another point, Montaigne might help us with self-acceptance. It can sound trivial, but Montaigne had a terrible memory: he was always repeating stories to his friends because he couldn't recall who he'd already told the anecdote to. He had key lines from his favourite authors inscribed on the ceiling beams of his study because otherwise he wouldn't be able to remember them. A poor memory isn't everyone's problem, but for some people it's a source of deep embarrassment and creates a feeling of inadequacy. It's reassuring to have a great figure from the past admit to the same problem.

At the same time, this nudge towards a less persecutory picture of our own failings is intertwined with another therapeutic concern: intimacy and the treatment of loneliness. We can feel close to Montaigne because he is so willing to be candid with us: he opens his vulnerabilities to our inspection.

Then again, we might be struck by the way Montaigne ponders issues. Often he doesn't seem to reach any definite conclusion: he tries out various ideas, sees their point, but isn't entirely convinced. He ushers us into the mental space in which we can think without feeling pressured to decide. We can let numerous different possibilities permeate our minds. We can let ourselves hold back from deciding what we think. And while decisiveness can be a virtue, being able to let an issue percolate in our minds may eventually lead to a wiser insight.

On this basis, we could be allowed to be confused about where exactly to place Montaigne on the therapeutic shelves. Does he go in the section on self-acceptance or in that devoted to friendship? Should the *Essays* be placed alongside books that offer reminders of basic truths or in the company of those that can assuage our loneliness, or of those that invite us into expansive reverie around complex problems?

There may be no precise answer to this question. In what follows, therefore, we have considered books on the basis of quite a traditional categorisation – that is, according to genre: history, novels, poetry, memoirs and so on. In each instance, we pick out a central therapeutic move that the work offers. But, as with the *Essays*, every great work for *us* ultimately offers multiple cures, or helps, for the troubles and sorrows of our souls.

Across a year, or a decade, or indeed over the whole of our lives, we will perhaps only engage fully with a few books. The ones that become our best companions will, like a rare and genuine friend, touch our deeper needs at many different points. The same book, like the same person, may be able to console us or to steel our courage; it may ease us towards new enthusiasms or edge us away from unhelpful preoccupations; it will be with us in our sorrows and want to help what is best in us to flourish.

A library can, of course, be physical: actual books on real shelves. But at its most important it is something entirely different: it is the works that live in our own minds, that accompany us in our thoughts even if we haven't opened their pages for a decade. They live in us and because they do, our own lives are less isolated, less confused, more expansive and more profound than they would have been if we had struggled on our own.

One last point before we turn to the books themselves: it is rare that everything in any book, no matter how well regarded by others, is helpful to us. To be a good reader means being ready to abandon a work in the name of that always more interesting and important volume: the book of ourselves.

I.
Philosophy

Roman mosaic panel with seven
philosophers, the so-called 'Academy
of Plato'

*We rarely notice how vague many of our
ideas are until we ask ourselves what we
really mean by a favourite word.*

Plato,
The Republic, c. 375 BCE

In conversation with others – and particularly in the conversation we have with ourselves in the privacy of our own minds – we constantly draw on huge notions like happiness, authenticity, justice, art, success or love. These words represent values we try to build our lives around. Yet if we ask what we really mean by them – if we try to define them clearly and carefully for ourselves – the mind typically goes blank. We know they matter, yet we can't pin them down. These represent the big ideals of existence, yet we realise we don't actually know what we mean by them.

The person who first drew attention to this disturbing paradox was Socrates, the mentor and friend of Plato and the central character in *The Republic*, which was written in Athens around 375 BCE.

The Republic recounts an ideal conversation, which goes on all evening and through the night, between Socrates and a few friends and companions, in which they try to work out what the notion of justice really implies. Gradually, they home in on the thought that justice must result in a better situation – otherwise an unjust society could be better than a just one, which is absurd. The discussion of justice leads to an even more difficult question: what makes one society better than another? Could equality be a central factor? Not on its own, because a society where everyone is equally poor or equally miserable doesn't seem admirable. Eventually, Plato makes Socrates say that justice involves strengthening the noblest, most intelligent and rational part of each individual.

The point isn't whether we agree with this conclusion or not. The value of *The Republic* is the way it shows how a serious and productive conversation can be developed and sustained.

Plato teaches us that defining our ideas properly is a complex, long-term task; we won't accomplish it easily or quickly, so we need not panic if we don't make headway at first. Recognising that we're unclear is, in fact, a constructive step.

We can try out an option: perhaps justice is … or love is … and we put the suggestion to the test. What counter-examples might there be? What objections might a friendly critic raise? We're trying to tease out some part of the larger truth this idea might be gesturing at. Plato tries to get us away from the picture of discussion as competition, in which each side tries to prove they are right, towards a mutual search for clarity.

As so often, with a book that is truly important to us, the focus isn't so much on grasping what the writer thinks as on learning from the writer's approach to explore and develop our own thoughts. It's not what they thought that is so exciting, but what we, in their company, might come to think for ourselves.

Red-figure bowl decorated with
erotic scene, Greek civilisation,
6th century BCE

We don't think enough about what
genuinely gives us pleasure. Epicurus
was one of the first philosophers
systematically to investigate the
question of what can make us happy.

Epicurus,
Letters, 341–270 BCE

It seems strange, and even slightly insulting, to suggest that we might not know what gives us pleasure. But this is to ignore one of the odder – and utterly normal – features of human nature: the extent to which our sense of what is enjoyable is conditioned by broad forces in our society. Without our being much aware of it, our ideas about what is fun and exciting are influenced by the pressure to fit in with others, concern with status and powerful commercial interests. Thus a particular society may make the pleasures of watching a football match or ordering a special bottle of wine in a fashionable bar much more imaginatively available to us than the delights of contemplating a cherry tree in blossom or tidying the kitchen.

The social reinforcement of certain activities can swamp the more delicate, and often not entirely clear, signals coming from deep within our own minds about what, in fact, delivers fulfilment – which may be very different.

One person is on our side: the Ancient Greek thinker Epicurus (341–270 BCE). He studied in Athens at the philosophy Academy founded by Plato a generation before. But Epicurus was not so much focused on abstract intellectual matters; he wanted to put ideas into practice. He and a diverse group of companions pooled their resources and purchased a modest house and plot of land in the suburbs and set off to discover if they could work out how to live a genuinely pleasing life together.

In his *Letters*, Epicurus explains what they discovered via this experiment in living. They realised that friendship is foundational. Almost any activity if undertaken with a good friend can be enjoyable: weeding the garden could be delightful in the right company. They highlighted modest, undramatic satisfactions – good conversation, simple food, going for a walk – that leave us refreshed and energetic and don't lead to regrets. They judge a pleasure not only by its immediate intensity but also by its longer-term role in our lives.

They particularly valued a state of mind they called *ataraxia*: concentrated serenity or freedom from anxiety. Without this, our pleasures become hectic, fragile distractions. But when we're relaxed we can appreciate low-key satisfactions. The path to this pleasure-facilitating calm involves paring down our commitments and distancing ourselves from unnecessary social expectations. We don't try to impress others, so we don't need to worry what they think of us. We're not trying to make it to the top, so it doesn't matter if we don't. We only see the people we really like. We only talk about the things that properly concern us. We don't gossip, and we don't try to keep up with the news. We protect our souls from standard but unproductive agitations.

Plans to change the world often sound heroically difficult: we must give up this and that; we must struggle. Epicurus suggests we'll change not because someone is berating us, but because we're being shown the path to truly fulfilling activities.

Peter-Paul Rubens, *The Death of Seneca*,
1612–1615

*We worry so much about time because we
don't think enough about what we are
really trying to accomplish.*

Seneca,
On the Shortness of Life, 49 CE

Our own mortality terrifies us. Youth is fleeting; we're middle-aged before we know it; old age is looming. The modern response is to try to prolong life: if we get everything right, we might add a decade or two. But close up we're still in a panic; the weeks and months still slip away.

Lucius Annaeus Seneca, known as Seneca the Younger (since his father also gained fame as a writer), takes a radically different approach: it's not how long we live that matters but what we do now, with the time we happen to have.

Seneca is a poignant guide because his own adult life was incredibly insecure. Born into a prominent family in Spain in 4 BCE, he built a successful career as a playwright, a financier and a politician. His success led him into the orbit of the ruthless imperial family: he became tutor and then adviser to the horrifically unstable Nero. He knew that his life could be cut short at any point by a rumour spread by a rival or by the vindictive whim of his employers.

Seneca's beautiful, powerful idea is that time is subjective. In ten minutes we could jot down the best idea we've ever had; in an hour we could have the most wonderful conversation of our lives; or we could fret away a weekend in sullen resentment. A day could be a huge intellectual, moral and imaginative adventure or it could be a blur of busy preoccupation with things, and people, that ultimately we don't care about.

A life cannot be measured by how many days it contains, but only by what went on in our minds during those days.

Seneca proposes that we waste our lives because we're afraid of what others would think if we were to concentrate on what is really important to us: we'd make less money; quite a few acquaintances would deem us fools; we'd probably never achieve any public acclaim (for that requires massive attention to what happens to please strangers). A life feels short because it is governed by timidity.

The irony is that we're actually tougher than we imagine. Seneca himself had a small room set aside in his grand home, furnished with straw to sleep on and provisioned only with bread and water, where he would often spend the night, teaching himself that he could manage with little, if he had to, and therefore not to fear what others would call disgrace or failure.

Touchingly, his essay on the topic is itself extremely short – a handful of pages. It's the same idea: if we can work out what we want to say, why should making a book longer be our objective; if we can work out what we love and esteem, why should the number of years we live be the way we judge our existence?

We become obsessed with quantity (how many words, how many years) when we are too frightened to focus on quality (how good, how important). Quality over quantity is the solution to our dread.

Avicenna (or Ibn Sina) teaching his
pupils, miniature from a 17th-century
Persian manuscript

*What are we really looking for
when we search for love?*

Abu Ali ibn Sina (Avicenna), *A Treatise on Love,* c. 980–1037 CE

Love is, perhaps, the most prestigious word in our cultural vocabulary. But it rarely strikes us that we need to ask ourselves what we mean by love and why we esteem it.

Abu Ali ibn Sina was born around 980 CE near the city of Bukhara in what is today Uzbekistan but was then part of the Persian Empire. As a child he excelled at memorising the Quran, to which he remained profoundly devoted all his life. His education also included a major engagement with Ancient Greek philosophy; in addition, he studied and later practised medicine. Even during his lifetime, his many writings were greatly admired not only in the Islamic world but in Christian Europe as well. He came to the notice of prominent political figures and passed much of his life as a roving adviser to a series of regional potentates.

In the *Treatise* he argues that love is a central element of all existence: a dog loves to run freely, a bird loves to fly, a tree loves to bring forth its blossom and fruit and to fill the woodland with its progeny. Even stones love: they love to be stable, they love to be well used – a block of sandstone, he says, yearns to be carved into an elegant arch. It may seem fanciful to talk of the romantic longings of a rock, but he is making a point that speaks directly to our own hopes and sorrows.

Like all creatures, indeed all things, we too yearn to be our best selves, to exercise the finest and happiest parts of ourselves. We yearn to blossom beautifully and to produce our finest fruit like a tree. But also, like a stone, we long for someone to come along and help us: the stone needs someone to shape it and place it at the point where its qualities are ideally valuable.

We love another person, he says, because we *hope* (even if we never put this hope explicitly into words) that they will help us become who we should be. They will prune us and chisel us; with their skill and guidance, we will flourish. We feel unloved when we can't find anyone who can provide us with this proper care and help. And *to love* is to wish to do this for another.

He offers us a moving and generous picture of our condition: our longings are essentially beautiful and noble but we are tragically confused in our conduct. We neither find nor give true love because we are not clear enough about what we are seeking or trying to offer. The task of a philosopher, as he sees it, isn't to change our nature but to help us see more clearly the good that is in us, in everyone and in everything and, through gentle, enticing guidance, to bring to the surface the longing to be the sweetest, kindest and most fruitful versions of who we are.

Ministry of Transport.

THE

HIGHWAY CODE

**Issued by the Minister of Transport
with the authority of Parliament in
pursuance of Section 45 of the
Road Traffic Act, 1930.**

LONDON:
PRINTED AND PUBLISHED BY HIS MAJESTY'S STATIONERY OFFICE
To be purchased directly from H.M. Stationery Office at the following addresses:
Adastral House, Kingsway, London, W.C.2; 120, George St., Edinburgh;
York Street, Manchester; 1, St. Andrew's Crescent, Cardiff;
15, Donegall Square West, Belfast;
or through any Bookseller.

1931.

Price 1*d*. net.

55-166

The Highway Code, cover of first
edition published in 1931

*Why have a code only for highways,
when so much of the damage we do to
one another occurs everywhere else?*

Departmental Committee on the Regulation of Motor Vehicles (UK), *The Highway Code*, 1931

At first sight it seems as unliterary and lacking in charm or drama as a book can possibly be. Yet this bland-looking document, drawn up by the UK Departmental Committee on the Regulation of Motor Vehicles at the Ministry of Transport and first published in April 1931, is one of the major inspirational and imaginative triumphs of writing.

Around most of the great tasks of life – how to find a partner, how to live a married life, how to raise a family, how to pursue a career, how to face our mortality – we are left to our own devices. It is up to us to work out, as best we can, what we should and shouldn't do. We make endless mistakes, we perhaps acquire a little wisdom but we generally fail to pass it on, and the next generation faces the same enormous challenges without the benefit of any accumulated, lucidly organised and authoritative guidance.

But there is one suggestive exception: driving. In many countries, you cannot take control of a car until you have demonstrated a thorough acquaintance with The Highway Code. It would be like saying no one was allowed to get married until they had passed a rigorous marriage test or that children could only be brought up by people who had carefully studied the family code.

Some of the code informs road users of legal requirements, but much of it simply states what drivers *should* do. Section 103, for instance, speaks of the use of indicator lights:

Signals warn and inform others of your intended actions. You should always

- *give clear signals in plenty of time*

- *make sure your signals will not confuse others. (If, for instance, you want to stop after a side road, do not signal until you are passing the road. If you signal earlier it may give the impression that you intend to turn into the road.)*

This specific instance is only to do with roads, yet 'indicating' is universal: there are marriages, friendships and careers that could have been saved by early signalling and an alert awareness of the possibility that the other may misinterpret our intentions, however clear they may be in our own heads.

The guidance the Code offers isn't merely the personal opinion of the writers; it represents the carefully considered analysis of why things tend to go wrong (the original committee learned much from The Royal Society for the Prevention of Accidents, a body whose actual scope does not quite live up to the sublime promise of its name).

In the ideal world of the future, the kindest, most imaginative and cleverest people would be set to work producing a multiplicity of codes for (perhaps) politeness, conversation, parent–child interaction, spousal disagreements and holidays.

Although The Highway Code is always telling us what we should or must (or must not) do, its cumulative effect is liberating: by being wisely alert to the causes of accidents it sets us free to go, independently, where we want, without causing any unnecessary carnage along the way. It is a promise of less accident-prone lives. All books should learn an essential lesson from it.

Edvard Munch, *Friedrich Nietzsche*, 1906

We make a great investment in things
without asking the prior question: what
do we really want from them?

Friedrich Nietzsche,
On the Use and Abuse of History for Life, 1874

Born in 1844, in Saxony, into a respectable though modestly wealthy family, Friedrich Nietzsche received a conventional scholarly education. He attended Schulpforta, a prestigious, though rigid, boarding school, and was a brilliant student at the universities of Bonn and Leipzig. In his early 20s, he was appointed to a professorial post at the University of Basel in Switzerland.

In 1874, when he was around 30, Nietzsche became obsessed by a powerful question, which is normally sidelined: what is scholarship – or indeed anything that is given high cultural status – actually for? He takes the things we're normally expected to admire *for their own sake* and asks about their real value in our lives.

It's one of the great dramatic moments of intellectual history. Nietzsche simply looked around and saw his colleagues, who were immensely learned about history or philosophy or who knew every detail of every work in the art gallery, and he asked the seemingly childish but urgent question: what's so good about knowing all that, especially if it doesn't make you (or others) exciting, wise, kind, generous, playful or even happy?

It's the same today. We don't ask properly what fame or wealth or fashion or social status are for. More intimately, we don't enquire what friends are for, or a party, or a marriage, or a long life, or travel, or reading lots of books.

Nietzsche's question isn't cynical. It's not a disguised way of saying that these are worthless, pointless distractions. It's entirely genuine. He says that if we know what something is for – that is, if we know what we truly and genuinely want and need from it – we can start to engage with it properly. Few things are intrinsically good or bad; what matters is what we use them for.

It's slightly terrifying: modernity is deeply anxious around specifying profound goals. We want people to read more but are reluctant to say what they should read and why. We hope 'the arts' will prosper but don't want to decide what is noble or base, wonderful or idiotic in this field. We like it when people get married but hate to enquire how the union will genuinely promote the happiness of both partners.

We are addicted to means and phobic around ends. Yet, logically, we need to put ends before means. Reading is only as good as the effect on us of what we read; a gallery is only as good as the wisdom it promotes; prosperity is only as good as the human flourishing it engenders. But our world celebrates things and people because of their elevated place in the machine, rather than because of the good they produce.

We feel we have no right to judge for others. Who are we to define ends? It's a false modesty. The commercial world has no qualms. It's only kindly, sensitive, caring people who stay quiet about what is ultimately good and worthy: the idiots and the crooks have the field to themselves.

Judith Kerr, illustration from *The
Tiger Who Came to Tea*, 1968

*Our fears are not facts; we are stronger
and more resilient than we think; the
metaphorical tiger at the door may even
become a friend.*

Judith Kerr,
The Tiger Who Came to Tea, 1968

There are certain things in life that are genuinely frightening; things we should run away from as fast as we possibly can. Born in Berlin in 1923, Judith Kerr had a horrifically acute knowledge of true fear. When she was 9, the National Socialists threatened to arrest her father, a prominent Jewish journalist, and the family fled to the UK. This book – which she also illustrated and which was first published in London in 1968, when she was in her mid-40s – is, behind the scenes, a meditation on *unnecessary* fear.

Little Sophie and her mother are at home when an enormous tiger turns up. He doesn't say much, but he's obviously extremely hungry and thirsty because he eats all the food in the house and drinks all the milk and 'all the water in the tap'. He gives Sophie a ride on his back, then he politely, but silently, takes his leave. And that's the whole story – except for one thing. Daddy gets back shortly afterwards and, of course, now the family can't have tea, since there's nothing left. But that's OK. They go to the quietly bustling local high street, where the lights are coming on in the dusk, and have something nice to eat at a cosy cafe.

A *tiger*, we may say, is a *thought* that distresses us: a child may worry there's a monster under the bed; as adults we may privately dread the prospect of our 40th birthday, hosting a dinner party, a tedious administrative task or a school reunion. *To have a tiger to tea* is in effect to domesticate a potential fear: to learn to feel at home with it, to see what might even be nice or fun about it and to find simple solutions to the problems it may bring.

The tone of the book is the opposite of alarmist. Unlike the panicky voice in our heads, the situation is narrated in the simplest, calmest, most matter-of-fact way. Judith Kerr invites us to internalise maturity.

For us, as adult readers, the illustrations are part of the therapeutic strategy. Sophie and her family are emphatically modest and ordinary. There's no hint of social status or career success; they are just like everyone else. Theoretically we know this is fine but, in our hearts, we recoil from embracing such a description of ourselves. We might not go around announcing it to the world, but below the surface we're slightly terrified of not being special.

The ordinariness of their lives in the pictures is beautiful. The kitchen table, the chairs, the crockery, even their clothes, are surely inexpensive and yet they are lovely too. They are exploring the therapy of mid-20th-century fashion and design: elegance is uncoupled from cost; the homely can also be refined and stylish. Sophistication needn't be cold and can be for the many and not just the few. Art and philosophy, to put it generally, needn't intimidate us. Like the tiger, they can come to tea and be comfortable in the kitchen.

Ben Nicholson, *1943–45 (St Ives,
Cornwall)*, 1943–1945

*We don't have to agree with a writer:
a book can give us the push we need to
follow our own line of thought.*

Iris Murdoch, *The Sovereignty of Good Over Other Concepts*, 1970

The joy of Iris Murdoch is that she combines qualities that our society often wants to tell us are incompatible. She did this at a career level: she was both a professional philosopher at Oxford, devoted to the careful construction of rational argument, and a highly successful novelist, devoted to describing, and sympathising with, the often irrational spaces of individuals' inner lives.

We have to keep in mind what this means in a more personal way: a tender grasp of why we are all privately mad, coupled with a faith that slow, painstaking clarity can be enormously productive. The problem in our own lives is how to hold on to both sides. We become hyper-emotional and connect deeply with an awkward truth about being human, but we experience logic as our enemy. Or we become sticklers for reason and facts but find we get nowhere because we miss so much of the reality of other people's inner lives – and our own as well.

The Sovereignty of Good is thrilling because, in the span of a dozen pages, it tries to spell out an entire view of life.

Murdoch says we are by nature radically limited, self-centred and anxious creatures. We are embroiled in the intimate and often unresolvable dramas of our own inner lives.

She proposes the experience of beauty as a central release. She describes how on days when she is feeling anxious and bitter, she loses herself in observing a bird wheeling in the sky. The grace of its flight draws her away from her self-preoccupation. Or maybe a work of art holds our attention just because of its shape and colour. We exit ourselves and start to love something outside us. We don't do so because we're forced to or because we have been sternly told we must but because what we encounter is so engaging and delightful.

Beauty, Murdoch says, is goodness made loveable. We're seduced, gladly, from our pained self-preoccupation into a captivated admiration for something independent.

'Good', in the big, ideal sense of the word, is whatever we can learn to love unselfishly. Hence, for Murdoch, humility is the most admirable of virtues because it signals a willingness to see something or someone as more important than our own immediate concerns.

It is good when someone retracts from competitive hostility and says, frankly, that their rival has real merits; when we grasp that another might have hurt us for motives that are understandable, or when we can allow that we are no better than the people we despise. We remove ourselves from central stage.

We might not agree with Murdoch. It doesn't matter much. What might matter more is that we, like her, seek to define for ourselves what 'good' really means.

II.
Politics

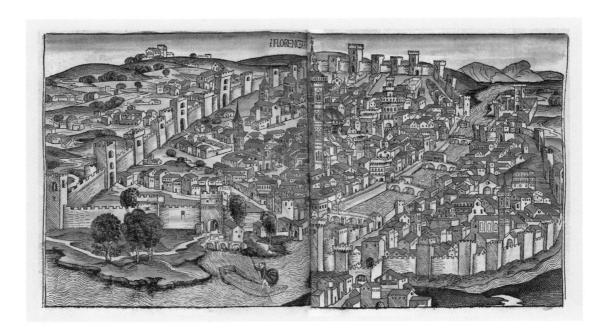

Wilhelm Pleydenwurff and Michael
Wolgemut, *View of Florence*, from Hartmann
Schedel, *Nuremberg Chronicle*, 1493

*If good people don't learn how to be
ruthless, bad people will always win.*

Niccolò Machiavelli,
The Prince, 1532

Niccolò Machiavelli was born in Florence in 1469, when the city was one of the richest and most powerful places on earth, but where his once-famous family had come down in the world. He, however, quickly rose to the top of the city's permanent officialdom, entrusted with major diplomatic missions and privy to the inner workings of government, until his career came crashing down in 1513, when he was in his 40s. He was, it seems wrongly, held responsible for a major policy failure. Machiavelli then retired to the country and wrote *Il Principe* (*The Prince*). Manuscripts soon started circulating, although the book wasn't officially published until 1532, some years after his death.

Machiavelli has become notorious for the stark brutality of his views. A prince – that is, the leader of a government – must be harsh. Showing mercy to opponents is often a mistake, as they will only take it as a sign of weakness. It is necessary to flatter and reward one's supporters; carefully hidden deceits of many kinds are central to maintaining power; be suspicious of everyone; strike first, with maximum force.

It sounds frankly barbaric: it's the opposite of how we ourselves would wish to behave and seems to cynically endorse the kind of conduct we deplore in the political figures we rightly despise

It's revealing, however, that Machiavelli dedicated his book to Lorenzo de Medici who, at the time of writing, was the heir apparent to Florence. Lorenzo was perhaps the most cultivated, intellectually sophisticated and artistically sensitive individual ever born to rule a major state. It's because Machiavelli wants wise and benevolent government that he thinks that the best people need to grasp without flinching what it will actually take to exercise and maintain power in the world as it happens to be. He wants the lovely, erudite, thoughtful

Lorenzo to be able to succeed; that's why his advice is so brutal: goodness is presupposed.

We may *wish* that gentle, pure souls could lead us, but in the crude arena of politics they will be easy prey. That is why it is so rare that sweet, sensitive and noble people ever attain the highest positions. Machiavelli also indirectly pleads that we forgive well-intentioned leaders their moments of skulduggery. If we turn on *them* for being less than perfect, we open the door to their much worse rivals.

More intimately, Machiavelli argues that across life in general, we need to face the grim realities of competition. A film-maker, for instance, can't just be high-minded in intent: they also have to bring in a wide audience, which inescapably means a degree of pandering to lower enthusiasms. A poet may need to court controversy to find a public for their more delicate and refined thoughts. And we ourselves may have to embrace a slightly stiffer defence of our own interests – to be more assertive, more calculating, more slyly diplomatic, more ready to tell a white lie – so that what is genuinely good in us can flourish in the radically imperfect world in which we have to live.

Olaudah Equiano.

or

GUSTAVUS VASSA

the African.

Cornelius Tiebout, engraving of
Olaudah Equiano, 1791. Frontispiece in
*The Interesting Narrative of the Life of
Olaudah Equiano...*, edition published
in 1791

*The unexpected complexity of other
people's experience.*

Olaudah Equiano, *The Interesting Narrative of the Life of Olaudah Equiano*, 1789

The notion of stereotypes has undergone a strange history. For a long time, to stereotype someone – to take one feature about them as the guide to everything they are – was considered very wrong (though, of course, it went on a lot). But it's come back in a new guise: a person who 'belongs' to group X is expected to think and feel a certain way. It's not always intended as hostile; indeed, at times, it's meant to be supportive.

A way to sidestep this is to immerse ourselves in the life story of an individual such as Olaudah Equiano. He was born in 1745, in what is now southern Nigeria, into a prosperous family. His origins, he speculates, may have been Jewish, given certain similarities between Jewish systems of belief and the social culture he grew up with. His father, as he records, was 'a gentleman who possessed numerous slaves'.

He had a carefree childhood until he was kidnapped by two ruffian men and a woman and sold to a tribal chieftain living nearer the coast. From there he was sold on and transported to the West Indies. There, he was appalled by the brutality and cruelty of the treatment of enslaved people. But his own merits were recognised by the captain of an English trading ship, who befriended him and then hired him from his master as a sailor. The bulk of his wages went to his 'owner', but he was allowed to keep a small percentage. Eventually, out of his minuscule resources, Equiano began trading on his own account, buying a trinket in one port and selling it at a profit at the next. After several years, at the age of 21, he was able to buy his freedom by, in effect, 'purchasing' himself from his master.

He sailed the world as a free man. He visited Turkey and Portugal, he was involved in shipwrecks and terrible storms, he returned to Jamaica and, with the help of an Indian prince, set up a plantation and became himself, briefly, a slave owner.

Finally, he made his way to England. He became a Christian and was ordained as a minister in the Church of England, with the idea (which never bore fruit) that he would become a missionary in Africa. He did, however, work for the British government on a project for repatriating liberated slaves, for which he was substantially rewarded.

His memoirs were published in 1789, the year of the French Revolution. Those who funded the publication of his book in London included the Prince of Wales, several dukes and a string of notables. The book was very successful and had a powerful effect on the growing abolitionist cause. Equiano married an English woman, with whom he had two children. He died in 1797, aged 52.

He had been an enslaved person, but the story of his life is also the story of his Jewish heritage, his slave-owning family, his adventures, his friendships, his business ventures as a plantation owner, his Christian zeal, his relations with the establishment and his happy marriage. It is about as unconventional a life as could ever have been envisaged; it's an essential story of freedom.

John Keenan, *Portrait of Mary
Wollstonecraft*, c. 1787

*Rights, ideally, are deserved,
not just given.*

Mary Wollstonecraft,
A Vindication of the Rights of Woman, 1792

It sometimes feels as if our world is obsessed with rights. Some people claim a right to free speech, even if what they say is manifestly idiotic; others claim a right not to be offended, even if they seem exceptionally thin-skinned; we have a right to vote, even if we vote for a buffoon. Has something gone wrong with how we think about rights?

One person who would certainly reply 'yes' was Mary Wollstonecraft. Born in London in 1759, she received what she later called a 'fashionable' education: one that sought to mould her to the feminine expectations of the era and so taught her nothing of science, economics, mathematics or logic. Neither, she laments, was she taught about self-discipline, how to make difficult decisions or how to make her way in a competitive and complicated social world.

In her late 20s Wollstonecraft worked briefly as a governess in an aristocratic household in Ireland and wrote a book on the education of young girls, stressing the importance of developing into realistic, rational, independent and kind individuals. In 1789 she visited France, then in the grip of revolution, where she had a tempestuous affair. She then returned to London to try out various (unsuccessful) 'experiments in living' – a commune with her female friends, a three-way relationship with the prominent artist Henry Fuseli and his wife – and to write her most famous work: *A Vindication of the Rights of Woman*.

She very much wanted women to have more rights – to run businesses, to vote, to become lawyers and legislators. But at the same time she saw most women as obsessed with fashion and preoccupied with male attention. (She was very hard on most men as well, who were boorish, dull and witless, in her estimation.)

Her point is this: a good society would have massively more equality and a huge extension of rights for women, but that would be because far more people were reasonable, diligent, prudent and willing to hone their talents. She had no enthusiasm for the notion that someone should be entrusted to elect the government, or be allowed to sit in parliament or conduct a legal case simply because of their sex; these rights should be linked to ability. It was abhorrent that such privileges were freely extended to talentless men, but the solution (as she saw it) couldn't be to extend them on the same lax terms to women.

Her vision is challenging: she longs to find people who combine strong rationality and emotional depth: these are the people, whether male or female, she wants in positions of responsibility. Universal rights can't get us there.

Eventually, Wollstonecraft found a brief period of happiness with a philosopher called William Godwin. They married and had a child, but in complications following the birth she died of an infection. She was only 38. Her daughter, Mary, went on to marry the poet Percy Bysshe Shelley and to massively eclipse her mother's carefully argued work by writing the renowned horror novel *Frankenstein*, published in 1818.

Auguste Rodin, *President Sarmiento*,
modelled 1896–1898; cast 1925

A strong voice for delicate things.

Domingo Faustino Sarmiento,
Facundo: Civilisation and Barbarism, 1845

It is a perverse feature of human societies that noisy, brash assertion easily drowns out serious, subtle thinking: a witless loudmouth can dominate a discussion, while a sensitive, thoughtful person struggles to be heard. Seriousness and refinement tend to lead to uncertainty. We want to do justice to complexity and nuance; we hesitate, consider and reconsider, while the brazen individual has no qualms: they boldly assert.

Domingo Faustino Sarmiento, a 19th-century Argentinian schoolteacher and journalist, saw this contrast of personalities as central to politics. He was from a poor but cultivated background, and a traumatic, decisive moment of his childhood occurred when a group of thuggish figures swaggered into his hometown. He was horrified that a small number of confident louts could hold such sway over a much larger number of decent but unassertive locals. Their minds were empty, their behaviour was vulgar and grotesque, but they could rule because sensitivity is weak and gentle.

In his mid-30s Sarmiento stood as a candidate in the presidential elections. Rather brilliantly, as his manifesto he wrote a biography of his principal rival, Juan Facundo, whom he saw as an essential representative of all the forces of barbarism.

This Facundo wasn't a lowlife brute; he was a wealthy landowner from an aristocratic family, but he'd never read a book and openly despised learning and culture, which he regarded as alien imports from Europe. He saw politeness as hypocrisy; the only thing that mattered in his eyes was how much money, land and cattle a person possessed. At one dramatic moment, Sarmiento was briefly seized by some of Facundo's supporters; thinking they were going to murder him, he declared: 'You cannot kill an idea.' He has fun imagining Facundo's

query when this assertion was reported back to him: *what's an idea?*

It took another twenty years for Sarmiento to succeed in his ambitions. He was finally elected president in 1868 and over the next six years he set about his civilising mission. He rapidly extended the school system, giving particular emphasis to education for girls. He built theatres and opera houses and libraries. He tried to build up a culture of conversation, good manners and elegance. He sponsored massive building works in the capital, Buenos Aires, taking Paris as the model of what a city should look like.

Across his whole life, Sarmiento tried to unite sensitivity with strength. He wanted us to love beauty *and* stand up for it; to be gentle and yet ready to do battle. He envisaged a world where the powerful would be tender and the cultured sturdy. He speaks, in effect, to the bullied parts of ourselves. He wants us to be proud of our refinement, our sensitivity and our grace and to insist on their universal validity.

His brilliant move is to identify barbarianism in the elite. Culture isn't a sly name for the preferences of the ruling class – it's the thing the powerful thugs lack and are afraid of. Refinement should come out of the shadows and rule the world.

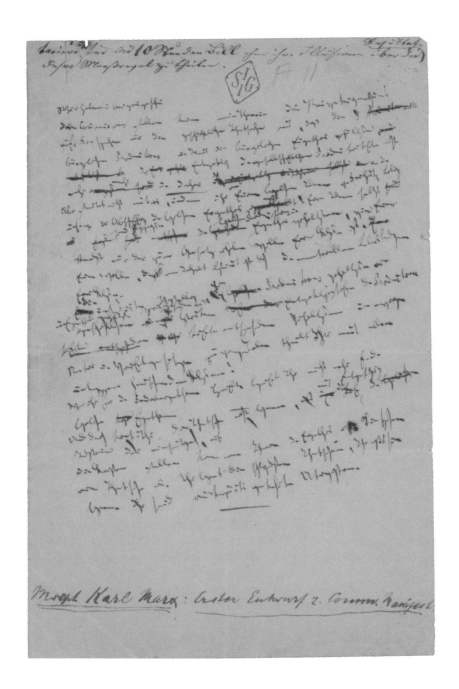

Karl Marx, the only surviving page of
the draft of the Communist Manifesto,
late 1847

One of the beguiling, but often
unrealised, possibilities of friendship
is that we might undertake a project
together.

Karl Marx and Friedrich Engels, *The Communist Manifesto*, 1847–1848

On 28th August 1844, Karl Marx and Friedrich Engels, who were both in their 20s and only very slightly acquainted, met at a fashionable café in Paris; over beer and conversation they became lifelong friends. They might have seemed an unlikely pair. Marx was messy, almost slovenly; he could be fierce and stern, and was always short of money. Engels was elegant; he was a good fencer, a fine horseman, a great party-giver and open-handed with his inherited wealth. But they discovered that they shared a deep sense of outrage at the conditions of the world they knew: not just the cruel poverty of so many but the stifled marriages and the dreary, narrow lives of the 'respectable' people they had each grown up among.

They took their friendship and their outrage seriously. Instead of merely talking over drinks or dinner, they considered how to spread their ideas and put them into practice. Out of all this grew *The Communist Manifesto,* which they wrote together in Brussels over a few weeks, from mid-December 1847 to late January 1848. Marx, characteristically, was sloppy and distracted until coerced by a strict deadline.

The book was hardly a great success. They had a limited number of often eccentric adherents; they were entirely dismissed by the educated, polite world to which they both belonged by birth and education. Our attitude to what they wrote is, understandably, distorted by what happened later, since the Manifesto can now be seen as a spur to Stalin's purges and Mao's appalling Cultural Revolution. And their central project – the abolition of private property – seems entirely unlikely to bring about the results they hoped for.

When they wrote it they had no idea of the fate of their ideas. They didn't feel as if they were telling world-dominating figures what to do. They were marginal, far from the levers of power; they were just two friends, excited by the same ideas.

It was a very sweet friendship. Each seemed to complete and balance the other; there was little rivalry. Marx was brilliant but unreliable; Engels was industrious and calm. And Engels was enough in love with his friend to let Marx's name predominate, even though he himself did a considerable amount of the writing and thinking; it wasn't even a sacrifice because he thought in terms of 'us' rather than 'me'.

It can seem almost wicked to regard one of the world's most consequential documents primarily through the lens of friendship. Yet from a therapeutic point of view this makes perfect sense. Our need in life isn't to plot the complex, imperfect lines between the Manifesto and what actually happened later in the Soviet Union. But how we imagine friendship is crucial to our existence. How can we collaborate with someone whose company we find charming? How can we see our differences as strengths to be combined? How do we let each other off the hook when it comes to weaknesses and limitations? How do we say 'we' rather than 'me'? How do we use kindness as a springboard to a better world?

John Ruskin, *The Northern Arch of the*
West Entrance of Amiens Cathedral, 1856

What kind of economy makes us happy?

John Ruskin,
Unto This Last, 1860

John Ruskin was one of the great intellectual figures of the 19th century. He was born in London in 1819, the only child of deeply devoted parents. His father was a successful and respectable wine merchant. From an early age, Ruskin wrote beautifully and powerfully about the arts; he was a tireless teacher and advocate of all that he thought was missing from the rapidly developing economies of the mid-1800s. As he aged he moved from art criticism to social criticism.

The essays that make up this book were first published, across six months in 1860, in *The Cornhill Magazine* – one of the grandest and most prestigious periodicals of the era. They were so hated by the readers, however, that the editor (who rather admired them) had to terminate the series. The plain cover of the first edition, in which the essays were collected as a book, gives no hint of the fireworks of the text.

Ruskin asks about *what* we value. Suppose, he says, a society, in the grip of a superstition, elected to put all its resources into building an immense pyramid of gold – perhaps to appease a vengeful god – neglecting education, their homes, the welfare of the elderly, the quality of their diet and the elegance of their cities. An economist would have no problem with this. It's what these people happen to choose; the concern would only be to help them accomplish it as efficiently as possible. To Ruskin, this demonstrates a monstrous outlook. Such a society is tragic and disastrous – and it is, Ruskin hinted, a version of our own.

What we should value isn't such a mystery, argued Ruskin. In another book, he describes his first visit (around 1840) to the quiet French town of Amiens. The streets are all pretty; the people are dignified but friendly; the shops are 'uncompetitive': over generations they've evolved to sell what the local people need; there's no advertising; everyone works productively, but not too much; there are few people who could be called rich and even fewer who could be described as poor. There are no ugly suburbs; the town proper simply gives way to small farms; no one is striving to build a fortune (why would they?) and there's no lack of work for someone able to milk a cow or carve a statue.

Ruskin intuited that a great number of people would like to live this way and was aghast that 'modern economics' had not focused on helping us to reach this form of contentment but talked only of maximising the production of steel or lowering the price of shoddy trinkets. We kill ourselves to grow the GDP but don't judge the worth of what anyone spends their money on.

We've unnecessarily embraced economic theories that make a point of ignoring our true longings. So, in an abundant world, we feel anxious about our resources, dislike our work and live in ugly places. Ruskin understood with shocking clarity problems we're still only beginning to make sense of in our own times.

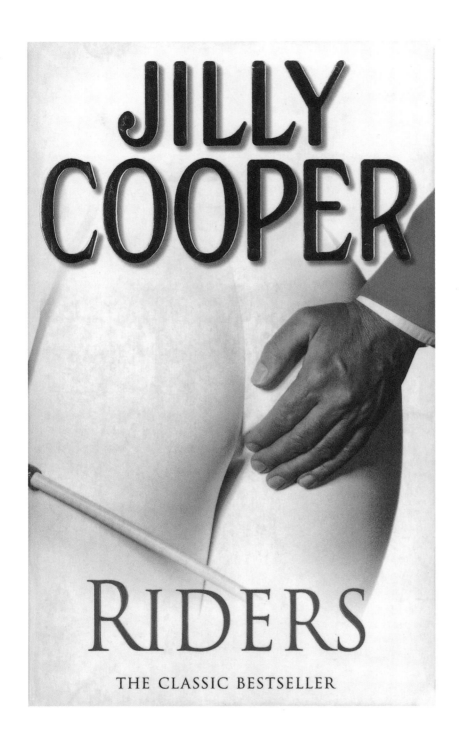

Jilly Cooper, *Riders*, cover of
edition published in 1986

*What are we to make of the sheer
popularity of 'trash'?*

Jilly Cooper,
Riders, 1985

When it was first published in the UK in 1985, *Riders* was often dismissed as *trash.* It's not too hard to see why. It's a story of the erotic passions and betrayals of shallow-minded, rich, aristocratic people who are all obsessed with horse racing. We are not invited to condemn this world but to revel in it. This was almost diametrically opposed to the settled vision of what serious literature should do: strip away the illusions of the bourgeois mind and reveal the stark horrors and psychological pain of reality.

What makes *Riders* essential political reading is not any insight it contains but rather the fact of its wide and enduring success. When asked in an interview how she felt about the disdain of the literary establishment for writers like her, Cooper remarked: 'they would rather like our sales figures'.

Cooper was touching on one of the great conundrums of culture: what is high-minded may be admirable but is statistically unpopular; what may be considered 'trash' is what the public, a lot of the time, actually prefers. We may often wish we could spend our evenings reading Dostoevsky, but we secretly find his masterpiece, *The Brothers Karamazov,* unmanageably dull. We might like to read Proust but find getting through *In Search of Lost Time* beyond our power. However, while in the bath or lounging at the airport, we find ourselves eagerly turning the pages of *Riders* or a similar work.

It can seem a rather bleak fact: human nature craves enjoyment and distraction – entertainment, in short – while brushing away the more difficult things we really should be concentrating on.

There is, perhaps, a fantasy solution – and one that may become technically available in time. Could we get a Jilly Cooper-type writer to redo the great works we guiltily abandon? We'd still have all the searing, dark truth of Dostoevsky, but rendered engrossing and fun. If Cooper had been able to give Proust a few writing tips, perhaps the extraordinary wisdom and beauty of Proust's mind would be more generally appreciated.

There is a self-destructive, but tempting, strain of puritanism that simultaneously (a) wants the truth to be painful and (b) laments the lack of public enthusiasm for the truth. This may suggest some naïvety about human nature.

The high goal of democratic government is to make what is good and true *popular.* But this involves admitting that Cooper knew something that eluded some of the great heroes of high culture: that we, the people, are very drawn to all sorts of things that 'theoretically' are *trash.*

Plato claimed that when kings are philosophers and philosophers are kings, all will be well on earth. A more democratic version might run: when the philosophers are populists and the populists are philosophers, some things will be a little better.

III.
History

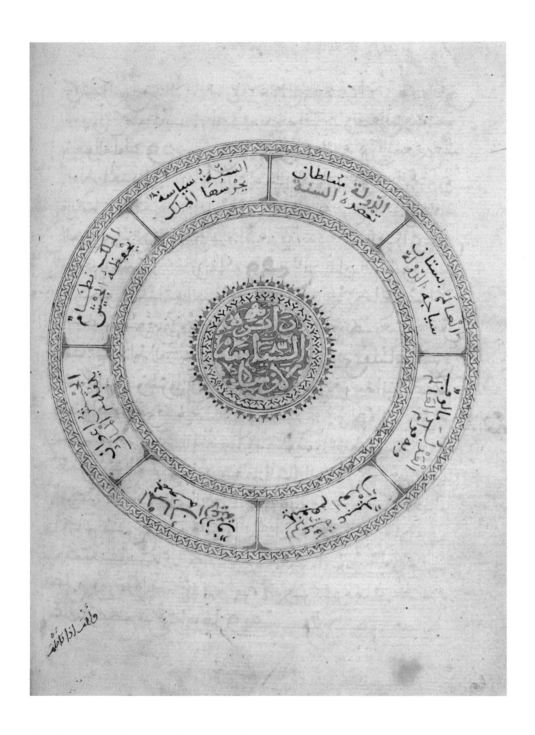

Ibn Khaldun, *Al-Muqqadimah*, 15th century;
table of contents listing kings and
rulers

*What does the past have to teach us
about how to live now?*

Ibn Khaldun,
Kitāb al-'Ibar, 1370s

The central reason for studying history is to learn from the mistakes and successes of past societies with an eye to applying these insights in the present in pursuit of wiser government. Although this approach might sound obvious, it is rarely pursued. The 14th-century North African writer and scholar Ibn Khaldun was, perhaps, the historian most devoted to this project. In the 1370s, when he was in his 40s, he published a history of the world entitled *Kitāb al-'Ibar* (*The Book of Lessons*).

Ibn Khaldun was born in 1332 into a distinguished family that traced their ancestry back to the time of Muhammad but by then resided in Tunis. He was highly educated, specialising in logic and philosophy as well as the close study of the Quran and of Islamic law. He held a series of senior positions as an adviser to local rulers across the whole of the western part of the Islamic Empire, though he found the endless factional strife depressing. He died in Cairo, in his early 70s, respected but marginalised.

Broadly, he was interested in the interplay between two key social forces: economic growth and solidarity or cohesion. His analysis of why states fail suggests that periods in which prosperity increases – when it looks as if the future is assured – are often quickly followed by disintegration. That's because overall prosperity becomes more and more unevenly distributed. Significant economic growth reflects substantial profit, which accrues to traders and owners of businesses. Such growth propels a society to regional prominence. It's suddenly richer and therefore more powerful than its neighbours, but at the same time massively divergent financial rewards for the few and the many undermine any sense of collective cohesion. There's a sense of 'us' and 'them' rather than 'we'. This makes a society vulnerable. It's ripe for another group to come along and try to win the allegiance of the disaffected majority. Thus societies where there is considerable inequality are inherently vulnerable to 'culture wars' – that is, to anxiety around what 'we' have in common.

Strikingly, Ibn Khaldun rejects one of the main modern responses: heavily redistributive taxation. That offers a way of reducing inequality, but it undermines growth since no one has much incentive to make substantial profits. There's no point in expanding a business if there won't be a personal reward. Instead, he believed that a certain kind of universally shared public religion was the solution, and it must do two things. First, it must stress spiritual equality: material success must be painted as something of a danger from a spiritual point of view. Second, it must make public charity a major, and revered, duty: the good thing about being rich must be that it's possible to help others. It's not the state disincentivising profit, it's religion redirecting profit to kindly purposes.

Despite being written almost 700 years ago, Ibn Khaldun's lessons often feel relevant. We've concentrated so much on growth, but we have barely started to think collectively about what generates social cohesion.

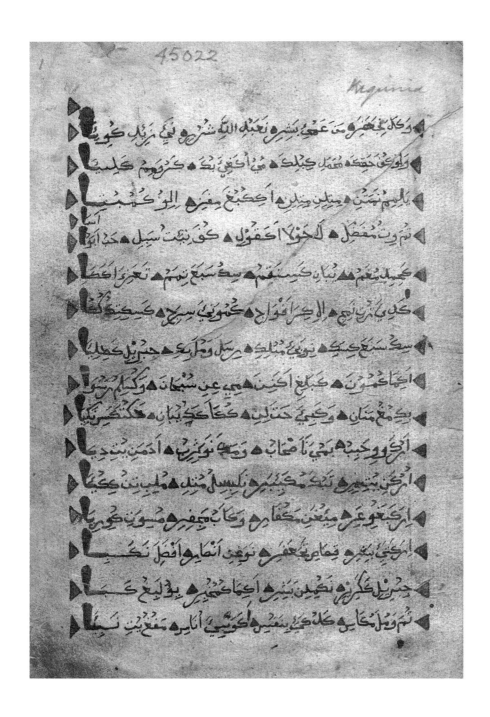

Mwana Kupona, a page from *Utendi wa Tambuka*, 1810–1860

We cannot judge our lives yet; what happens in the future will change our perspective in ways that we can hardly imagine.

Mwengo,
Utendi wa Tambuka, 1728

We're always looking back over our lives, often with dismay. What seemed like a great idea ten years ago now feels like a big mistake; we come to regret things we were once proud of. But our capacity for retrospection (to give it a name) can develop in more interesting and positive ways, and this fascinating book shows us how.

Utendi indicates a kind of poem, intended to be recited aloud, with a rich, easy rhyme scheme and a lingering pause at the end of each fourth line, ideal for drama and suspense. The *Utendi wa Tambuka* was composed in Swahili for the Sultan of Pate, a small coastal city-state in what is today Kenya. It tells of a battle that took place at the town of Tambuka (near the present border between Saudi Arabia and Jordan) more than a thousand years earlier, around 630 CE, when the newly emergent Islamic forces under the leadership of Muhammad first clashed with Christianity and the West.

The story begins when the Prophet Muhammad writes to the Byzantine Emperor Heraclius, asking him to renounce Christianity and accept the truth of Islam. The Emperor is supposed to have replied acknowledging that Muhammad was indeed the Prophet of God, but stating that, regretfully, he himself must abide by the traditions of his ancestors and remain a Christian. The Emperor's refusal induces Muhammad to attack the Byzantine outpost of Tambuka and the poem ends with its capture.

It was a minor military victory; the Islamic commanders at the time couldn't have known what it meant. The much later poem views the clash at Tambuka as prefiguring the vast expansion of the Islamic Empire, leading eventually to the capture of the Byzantine capital, Constantinople, in 1453 and then a drive into Europe, with a Muslim army reaching the gates of Vienna in 1683. We may imagine the poem being written at this point, on the threshold of seemingly decisive victory.

But reading it today, the perspective has shifted again. Three centuries after the time it was composed, the meaning of 'a battle' between Islam and the West is very different. And we don't know how that might change yet again in the future. The meaning of the battle of Tambuka keeps changing. Was it a decisive step forward or a fatal step down a path that would lead to ruin? Was it a portent of unending conflict, or will it be enfolded into a still longer narrative of eventual reconciliation and peace?

Such shifts in perspective apply to our own lives: a first date seemed wonderful and marked the start of an exciting relationship. Then things got difficult and that date began to look like a fatal mistake. Later we realise that we learned a lot through our mistakes and the date takes on a poignant significance. And we can't know how, in the end, we might view it from the perspective of a final hospital bed.

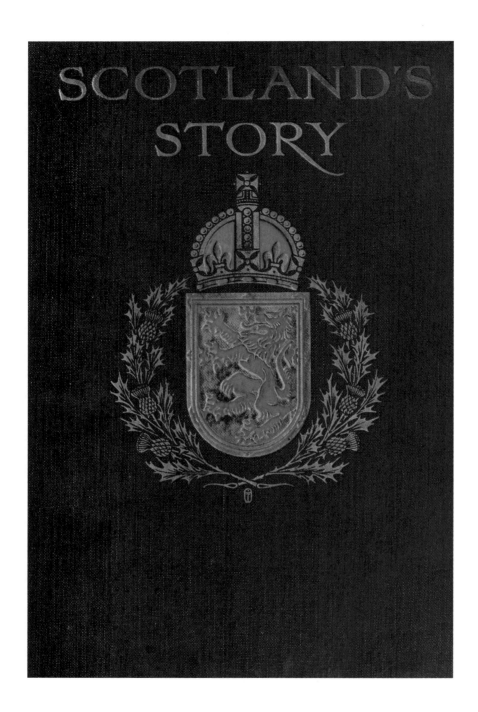

Henrietta E. Marshall, *Scotland's Story:
A History of Scotland for Boys and Girls*,
cover of first edition published in 1906

*We already know the worst, but we long
and need to be able to love and admire
as well.*

Henrietta Elizabeth Marshall,
Scotland's Story, 1906

There's an understandable preoccupation in the modern world to impress upon us just how wicked, corrupt and unjust the society in which we live really is and to trace these horrors back through our collective history. Anything we thought was fine can be shown to be tarnished; the individuals and institutions we might have hoped would deserve our devotion are inevitably revealed as venal and oppressive.

Scotland's Story, published in 1906 by the once popular but now forgotten historian Henrietta Elizabeth Marshall, is an attempt to write history in noble terms: it is always seeking glimmers of dignity and honour, even when things go wrong. It is quick to note moments of bravery and generosity; it stresses good intentions; if disaster strikes, we hear how it was recovered from; losses are mourned rather than condemned. It's nothing like the full, unvarnished story. It simply sets out to say: here are all the best, most admirable things about the history of Scotland. It's a project that, today, we are supposed to regard with hostility, and that is why it is helpful.

There's a powerful parallel between the way we view a society and the way we see ourselves as individuals. In general terms: do we need to know more about what is mean, wicked and cruel about ourselves? Perhaps some people do. But we, as the individuals we are, have an almost overdeveloped capacity for shame, guilt and regret. What we need is help with telling the story of our lives in less persecutory, less disastrous terms. We need to consciously seek out the little moments of dignity, the minor successes, the goodwill, the good intentions, the small kindnesses. We need to become the H.E. Marshall of our own story.

It is a tragedy that the contemporary cult of guilt strikes most deeply into the hearts of people who are already very committed to self-criticism and self-improvement, while those who perhaps should revise their outlook openly scoff at claims that they need to change. To think well of ourselves is not a self-indulgent, wilfully blind luxury. It's rather the required platform from which we can operate more successfully in the world.

Therapy is always personal. One person needs to become more aware of their flaws, another needs to become more aware of their merits. Some people need to puncture their pride, others need to build it up. In private, we are trying to find the way of telling our own version of *Scotland's Story* – one that gently reminds us that, for all our follies and imperfections, we are indeed ordinarily good people, deserving of love and respect.

Frances Partridge, *Dora Carrington,
Saxon Arnold Sydney-Turner*, Ralph
Partridge and Lytton Strachey, 1926–1927

*Lytton Strachey (in the straw hat),
lounging on a deckchair in the garden
of his beautiful country house with his
charming bohemian friends,* released
Eminent Victorians *in 1918 to huge
success.*

Lytton Strachey,
Eminent Victorians, 1918

Strachey was born in 1880 into a grand and prosperous English family. His father, Sir Richard, was a general; the Earl of Lytton, the godfather after whom he was named, was Viceroy of India. At Cambridge University he was a much-loved member of the ultra-elite and secretive Apostles: a group of the twelve most intellectually and socially distinguished undergraduates, who met on Saturday evenings to discuss ideas and eat sardines on toast.

Eminent Victorians, which Strachey worked on for several years and which came out shortly after his 38th birthday, was his masterpiece: in a quiet, funny and elegant way, it dismantles all that his parents' generation had assumed was centrally important.

In the book he selects four of the most revered characters of the previous era. His first target, Cardinal Manning, was the leader of the English Catholics: a brilliant administrator, string-puller, oily manipulator and (in Strachey's unbelieving eyes) an absurd character, devoting his life to an irrational figment. Next he turns his fire on the preposterous General Gordon, who, to vast public acclaim, extended the British Empire into the Sudan, guided, as he imagined, by obscure passages in the Old Testament. The third to be annihilated is Thomas Arnold, who had instigated a massive and utterly misguided reform of education, training up a generation of self-righteous military officers and colonial administrators. Finally, Strachey took aim at Florence Nightingale, who had (he admits) improved the nursing profession but who, while she advocated fresh air and exercise and equality as the cure for all ills, spent her entire adult life lying on a sofa in a darkened room in the most fashionable and exclusive street in London.

Strachey was right: they were indeed all bizarre characters, and his calmly vicious prose is delightful. But there's an extraordinary irony to his project. To us, he too is a strange and exotic individual. He, like those he excoriates, is a creature of *his* time: aloof (he often lamented the shortcomings of 'ill-bred' persons), privileged and narcissistic (he was immensely proud of his chestnut-coloured beard), his knowledge of 'real life' was limited to occasional trysts with postmen and burly gardeners.

But it is Strachey's own vulnerability to precisely the same attack he unleashed on others that makes his book so important and poignant. *Every* generation deserves to be shown up in its weakness and to be condemned for its sincerely intended stupidity. The same will apply, inevitably, to our own times. The people who are righteous *now* will strike the intelligentsia of the future as buffoons and pedants; their most ardent convictions will look demented; their deepest values will seem trivial, embarrassing or cruel; their victories will look like defeats for civilisation. Strachey was an eminent Edwardian just a generation away from heartless ridicule.

We read Strachey when we are at odds with our times: the grander, unintended message of his work is that *all* times are mad. We are not unfortunate to live when we do; we are simply meeting the eternal madness of the world in its current guise.

Intermezzo:

A Note on Aesthetics

The Rime of the Ancient Mariner by
Samuel Taylor Coleridge, cover of
edition published by George Harrap
and Co. in 1910

*Some books understand our weary
reluctance to start reading: they
seduce our eyes and invite us to pick
them up and turn the pages just for
the sensuous pleasure of touch.*

Marcus Aurelius, *Meditations* (also known as *The Golden Book*), 161–180 CE

From a logical point of view, it shouldn't really matter what the cover of a book looks like: obviously, the most moving and helpful words could be contained within the most lurid covers. And yet, as physical creatures, our behaviour is influenced by visual aesthetics. A drinks manufacturer will search for the right, alluring shape of a bottle – though of course it doesn't alter the taste of the contents. Packaging is often deployed cynically, to make a product look more appealing than it really is. But if packaging can be used basely, it must also be possible to use it wisely: to lure us into taking hold of something that has a great deal to offer us.

This was the thinking behind a publishing venture launched around 1900 by a UK and India-based business, George Harrap and Co. The idea was to entice people to read the classics by publishing them as cheaply as possible in very beautiful editions.

They felt, for instance, that Marcus Aurelius' *Meditations* should be loved by many. In the 2nd century CE, Marcus Aurelius was one of the 'good' emperors of Rome, and across his life he kept a notebook of key ideas for purely personal use. One of the most touching and useful was that he set himself to meditate regularly on who he was grateful to. He wasn't trying to sum up a person, who may have had some pretty serious shortcomings; he simply spent time going over deliberately, and in great detail, the good they had done him and the lessons for which he was indebted to them. It's a very simple and benign technique.

But how to encourage tired business-people and busy parents to actually engage with, and embrace, the ideas of a long-dead figure whose life might seem to have nothing in common with theirs?

One thing the publishers hit upon was the texture of the covers. They used a soft, velvety green binding with elegant gold lettering. They thought a lot about scale as well: they chose a perfect size to hold in one's hand. It opens flat, the pages are creamy and thick; there aren't too many words on any page. The print is elegant; there are wide spaces between the lines. Everything is done to charm us – almost inadvertently – into starting to read. In a certain sense, we've been taken in by marketing tactics, but we've been taken into something noble, wise and helpful.

When it comes to reading, we need all the sweeteners and inducements we can get. After a demanding day we're often not going to feel in the mood for some moral instruction or an encounter with early 19th-century poetry. But the volume is so sweet-looking, so nice to run one's fingers over, that almost by chance we find we're glancing through a paragraph or an intriguing stanza and turning our minds to the life-guiding thoughts it contains.

BIBLIOTHÈQUE DE PHILOSOPHIE CONTEMPORAINE
FONDÉE PAR FÉLIX ALCAN

HÉRITAGE DE MOTS
HÉRITAGE D'IDÉES

PAR

Léon BRUNSCHVICG

Membre de l'Institut

PRESSES UNIVERSITAIRES
DE FRANCE

Léon Brunschvicg, *Héritage de mots,*
Héritage d'Idées, cover of edition
published in 1950

Just holding the book makes us feel ...

Léon Brunschvicg,
Héritage de mots, Héritage d'Idées, 1945

We've quite probably never heard of the author: Léon Brunschvicg was a professor of philosophy in Paris in the 1920s and 30s, and the supervisor of Simone de Beauvoir's graduate thesis. A distinguished Jewish intellectual, he wrote this particular book when, in his 70s, he fled to Switzerland following the Nazi occupation of France in 1940. It was written from the most poignant of motives: he realised he would never see his young granddaughter again. He longed to tell her what his life had been about and to pass on to her some kind of usable patrimony – his private thoughts on the ideas that had meant most to him: *experience, freedom, love* and *the soul*.

Movingly, in the final chapter, he writes to her about the difference between knowing someone face to face and the memory of them after they have gone when 'they can't any longer speak to us'. He tenderly implies that the dead are longing to speak all the time. They long for us to understand what they loved, to appreciate their confusions and uncertainties, to sense the honour of their mistakes and not to hate them for their failure in the face of historical forces that, in retrospect, we think they should have understood and defeated from the start. This is what he is trying to convey to his absent, beloved granddaughter. The essays weren't made public until the early post war years, by which time Brunschvicg was dead.

What may touch us, as much as or more than the text, is the physical character of the book. We imagine finding a copy, for the price of a croissant, in a neglected corner of a Parisian bookshop: the thin, plain grey-green cover takes us back to the epoch. It's sober and restrained, and merely announces the author's name and the title. It knows nothing of advertising: it can't shout; it wants to be loved and understood for what is serious and deep about it. It combines great modesty with ambition.

If we read the text, we might not quite grasp what Brunschvicg really wants to say; we may lose the thread of his elaborate discussions. But it's not really the details that we care about. When we hold this object in our hands we are, at an animal level, back in parts of the late 1940s. We're back with those who lived there, who were earnestly trying to be loyal to the best of the past. We're on the threshold of a new society where, perhaps, much that has mattered to us won't seem valid. Via our frayed, fragile, second-hand copy we're joining hands with something noble and tender in the past.

IV.
Religion

Krishna and Arjuna on a chariot, from the
Mahabharata, India, 18th-19th century

*Serenity achieved via philosophical
meditation.*

The Upanishads,
c. 600 BCE–1500 CE

Much of our distress is around what is happening now: we've got ten things to do and the boiler has stopped functioning; we've spilt red wine on our white trousers; our partner has just said something almost designed to upset us. Yet, oddly, we know that with time most of these frustrations will melt away. As time sweeps on they'll be submerged in the bigger picture. It always happens. Remember that time ages ago when our flight got cancelled in Canada and we got incredibly agitated? Now the anxiety feels like it happened to someone else. It's one of the most tantalising aspects of existence: we suffer now, yet we know that when we see these things from afar we won't care so much.

The Upanishads is the collective name for around 100 philosophical reflections, mostly originating in northern India between c. 600 BCE and 1500 CE. The ideas, which form the intellectual core of Hinduism, were transmitted orally for many generations. The name 'Upanishad' implies the intimate knowledge that is available only to those who are in personal, direct contact with a teacher.

Their therapeutic project is to instil in us a permanent sense of the entirety of the cosmos and the vast, endless ocean of time. The more this vision becomes native to us, the less the annoying incidents of life, which are tiny in comparison, will be able to disturb or distress us. Instead of being obsessed with here and now, we'll be attuned to always and everywhere – and much happier for it.

The Upanishads invite us to move away from immediate sensation to timeless thought. One meditation asks us to suppose that someone 'loves' sunshine. What do they really love? Not sunshine itself but the sense of life-giving power it stands for. So they really delight in an idea. And that idea is independent of the sun. Or, to take a modern version, suppose someone 'loves' fashion; what they really love is the sense of having a special appreciation of beauty. And that is much bigger than fashion itself. Everything that excites us now points to a larger, more timeless idea. A meditation gets us to focus on the idea. In fact, all religions and all art may be seen as attempts to do this, which is why Hinduism has, at times, claimed that everyone in the world is actually a Hindu.

All the outward features of Hinduism – the names of divinities, the myths and the rituals – are, ultimately, mechanisms for helping us reach a state of enlarged perspective in which we identify with the totality of the cosmos.

If The Upanishads were being written today, they might invite us to spend a lot of time thinking about subatomic particles and that we ourselves are constituted of material that was formed billions of years ago in exploding stars, from which point of view our malfunctioning boilers, stained trousers and sly comments from partners lose their power to distress. We are never far from needing reminders of cosmic totality.

立言不朽惠敷無疆貽燕令德
偉哉素王人倫之表帝道丕緜廠
功實茂具用矢臧叔中跂星盛典
載揚洪名有熱鑰範彌彰
源齊昭嚴書

晴川法眼養信筆

Kano Seisen-in Osanobu, *Portrait of So'o
(Confucius)*, first half of the 19th
century

*A loving tribute to our dignity as
middling people.*

Confucius,
The Analects, c. 479 BCE–220 CE

We won't make it to the top. We won't get to be in the circle of those who influence the fate of the world. But we're not complete outsiders either; our lives are outwardly respectable enough. It's an unromantic situation: we belong to neither the stratospheric few nor the downtrodden many. We hold positions of genuine but limited responsibility. We may spend our days looking after people's teeth, going through the legal fine print of a shipping contract or overseeing the marketing strategy for an interesting kind of cheese. What we do needs to be done, and it needs to be done well, but no one will write a soul-stirring ballad cheering on our endeavours.

But we do have one very great friend who appreciates what we do and the kind of people we are: the ancient Chinese scholar and teacher known as Confucius.

Born in China in 551 BCE, into a middle-ranking but not well-off family, Confucius had a long career in public administration, but he increasingly turned his attention to the education of aspiring bureaucrats. Compiled by his followers, *The Analects* (meaning 'chosen things') are a collection of the sayings and ideas of Confucius. As a book it only arrived in its current form about 700 years after his death.

In his teaching, Confucius was powerfully motivated by the insight that the state of Chinese society depended not so much on who was at the very top but on the character and conduct of those in subordinate positions. An emperor or a governor cannot rule alone: they depend on many others to give advice, to shape the terms on which decisions are made, to soften in practice a harsh edict or to reduce the negative impact of a misguided policy. They are the anonymous and yet central figures in how the world actually works.

In modern terms, Confucius insists that the collective good depends much more than we normally realise on large numbers of people being honest and professional in their work, in genuinely seeking the best for others, in learning from their mistakes and in passing on the lessons of their experience. Middling people, such as ourselves, cannot easily see our impact on the world because, individually, it may be small. But, Confucius says, collectively it is decisive.

At times we lament the seeming triviality of our lives. From a distance we might envy the firebrand or those who gain the great rewards. Confucius wants to change our minds: we are already, in our modest way, doing the work that makes the world work.

The Analects are a guide to a good mentality when we are neither at the top nor the bottom. More than that, they are one of the few great works of the world that specifically target and praise those who work quietly behind the scenes to ensure that there is a little less commercial fraud or gum disease, and a few more charming cheese platters, in the world.

Rembrandt, *Christ Preaching (La Petite Tombe)*, c. 1657

We can be loved as we are, if we learn to forgive others and ourselves.

The New Testament,
1st century CE

In our darker moments, we come face to face with the idea of our own failure: we'll crash financially, we'll arrive at a dead-end job, we'll let down those we most care about and give them reason to despise us, we'll be socially disgraced. We're terribly alone with our fears; we hardly even dare share them with our closest friends or our families. We will not only be unloved; worse, we will be *unworthy* of love. The power of the New Testament comes from the fact that it is addressed to these fears.

Written at various times during the 1st century CE, when the Roman Empire was at its height, the New Testament consists of four different but convergent accounts of the life of Jesus, a carpenter turned wandering preacher who had lived and died a few decades earlier in the province of Judea.

When, in the image above, Rembrandt imagined Jesus talking to people, he placed him not in the Middle East in ancient times, but in the sordid back streets of contemporary Amsterdam among people who have already failed. He was getting at the core point of the story: extending love to those who are considered (and who consider themselves) *unworthy* of compassion or kindness.

We don't need to believe in the historical reality of the events – or in any kind of Christianity – to be moved by the ideas the book advances, which are so at odds with the dominant values of the modern world.

There's a huge emphasis on forgiveness in the New Testament: 'Let he who is without sin cast the first stone' or 'Do not judge, lest ye be judged.' In other words, it is our awareness of our own frailty that can power the economy of compassion. We forgive because we know that we need to be forgiven.

The main characters in the story are humble: Jesus is a modest artisan; his close friends are simple fishermen; he spends time with prostitutes and thieves. Wealth and high social status are presented as unimportant in understanding a person's true worth. Jesus praises meekness and gentleness; he's more drawn to those who suffer than to those who are conspicuously successful.

The culminating point of all the stories is the absolute worldly defeat of Jesus. He is tried on trumped-up charges and executed as a criminal. His pitifully small band of supporters deny they have had anything to do with him and go into hiding. The point of all this is reassurance. It is to say 'However bad it gets for you, I know what it is like. I've been there. I've been utterly broken and defeated and outcast.' It's an astonishing idea: that it's when we're at our lowest that we are most worthy of love. It's no surprise that this is the book one reads in prison, in the psychiatric hospital and as we consider whether or not to jump off a bridge. It's a book designed to keep us on the side of life.

Two pages from the Quran, Islamic School,
17th century

*It's not how widely we read that
matters, but how deeply.*

The Quran,
610–632 CE

One of the odder features of modern culture is the belief that we should read as widely as possible. There are so many fields that we feel we should be informed about and so many books others have recommended. We are often haunted by the sense that we're not reading enough.

In Islamic culture, the Quran is *the* book. The words were sent, sentence by sentence, from God to the Prophet Muhammad around 1,500 years ago. Over a period of more than twenty years, he simply wrote down what God wanted the whole world to know.

The Quran, therefore, suggests a radical view of reading: there is only one book we truly have to read, and we should spend our whole lives absorbing and reflecting on its message. To deeply know and understand one book is more important than skimming our way through hundreds. We may end up committing large parts of this book to memory and feel no shame that we have scarcely opened another volume.

Though unfashionable, the underlying point is crucial. A great book brings us face to face with the considered thinking of a wonderfully intelligent and serious writer. It is an encounter that can (and perhaps should) last a lifetime. If we find in it assertions we want to disagree with, we are stimulated to frame our objections in terms that would make sense to the writer; we then *might* imagine what their replies to our comments would be. We enter into a deep dialogue. We ponder anything that doesn't seem to make sense, and we consider what it might mean. We apply the ideas we find in it to our daily lives; we test our experience against it; we find its phrasing and vocabulary slowly influencing our own; our minds end up being shaped by it.

We go back to the same book again and again, and we find that as we age we see new things in it, or it becomes poignant because it keeps alive aspects of our younger selves that we are otherwise losing sight of.

This means that across our lives we can properly read only a very few books, so finding them becomes important. They may not be initially the most exciting. They may not be page-turners, but a page-turner is designed to be read only once, and the cleverest cliffhanger means nothing once we know the denouement. The books that really touch us may be ones we slowly grow to love. They reveal their depths gradually; they are a little shy, so we need to be gentle, at first, in what we ask of them, but eventually they will become our dear friends.

The Quran is exceptionally beautiful and profound, but even if it isn't the one book we are devoted to, it sets the properly high standard for engagement. If a book is genuinely worth reading, it's worth reading many times. It might almost be the only thing we look at.

Joseph Mallord William Turner,
The Golden Bough, exhibited 1834

*Religious myths are technically false,
but can they also be important?*

J.G. Frazer,
The Golden Bough, 1890

We tend to feel disturbed by religion. We'd like to be respectful, but so many of the ideas sound bizarre and impossible. We don't want to be mean to friends, relatives or strangers who are devout, but how can we make sense of their apparent devotion to absurdities? *The Golden Bough* is the book to help us, for it explains how a conviction can be at once empirically false and yet profoundly meaningful and moving.

James George Frazer was born in Glasgow in 1854; he was a spectacularly diligent student, winning a scholarship to Cambridge and then a fellowship at Trinity, then the most prestigious and intellectual of the many colleges that make up the university.

Initially published in two volumes in 1890, Frazer kept adding to the text. By 1915 it had grown into an enormous twelve-volume set. It was the first very widely read study of myth and anthropology.

Frazer's interest is in shared myths: he's struck by how, across time and space, different societies have invented similar stories for themselves. There is the myth of 'the chosen one', which the title of the book obscurely alludes to. It refers to a tree, in ancient Roman stories, from which only one divinely appointed person is able to pluck a wonderful branch, made of gold. In Tibetan Buddhism, the Dalai Lama is revealed by fate, not selected by human competition. Likewise, in English myth there was supposed to be a sword stuck in a stone and only one person – the rightful king – could pull it out. In a modern version, in the *Harry Potter* stories, Harry is frequently named as 'the chosen one'.

For Frazer, this commonality suggests that it is the structure of the human mind that prompts such diverse communities to latch on to the same ideas. The ideas might not be true, but they are clearly important. We can critique them as unscientific, but we can't dismiss them as humanly worthless.

At the time of writing, England was officially a Christian country, and Frazer's most controversial argument was that Jesus, the god who sacrifices himself and is then resurrected or reborn, is a standard figure. The early Mesopotamian god Dumuzid is dragged by demons into the realm of the dead, but is eventually released, thus returning to the world of the living. In Egyptian myth, Osiris, the god of fertility, is killed and dismembered by his brother Set, the god of storms and violence. But the fragments of Osiris are put back together by the maternal goddess, Isis. All such stories, Frazer suggests, are retellings of a more ancient myth concerning the sun. The sun, which feeds all life, 'dies' in the autumn and is 'reborn' in the spring. Jesus fits a pattern, but it's a pattern that humans seem to need.

The religious may be empirically wrong in their beliefs, Frazer's book hints to us, but they are participating in the great collective and historical adventure of the human mind.

V.

Psychology

Théodore Chassériau, *François VI,
duc de la Rochefoucauld*, 1836

What might be good about being cynical?

François de La Rochefoucauld, *Maxims*, 1665

A disturbing lesson of experience is the discovery that pretty much everyone has some unpleasant, rather dark, secrets. In his *Maxims*, La Rochefoucauld is eager to detect and publicise the failings of human nature. He seems so mean.

He was born in Paris in 1613, into one of the most ancient noble families of France; he came into his dukedom and responsibilities – including active military command – when he was only 16. Though at the pinnacle of society, his expected political career did not materialise. He was of great behind-the-scenes service to the crown but was publicly brushed aside. He then supported an aristocratic revolt, known as the Fronde, against the youthful Louis XIV, but the insurrection was quickly crushed. In middle age he increasingly withdrew into private life.

From about 1660, when he was in his late 40s, La Rochefoucauld and a couple of distinguished friends developed a kind of literary game in which they would come up with 'ideal sentences' – a single line or two encapsulating a big, surprising and potent idea about life that reflected their own experience and their observations of others. Out of this long-running hobby, La Rochefoucauld developed his private set of around 500 short maxims, first published in 1665, with the final edition published in 1678, two years before his death. For instance:

14.   *People not only tend to forget benefits received from others; they are even prone to hate those who have helped them.*

That is: true gratitude is almost non-existent.

31.   *If we had no faults we should not take so much pleasure in noting those of others.*

In other words, if you meet someone who is very critical of others, you can be sure they have much to hide.

72.   *If we judge of love by the majority of its results it rather resembles hatred than friendship.*

Don't, therefore, envy 'loving couples'; they'll be secretly tormenting one another soon enough.

149.   *The modesty which pretends to refuse praise is but in truth a desire to be praised more highly.*

Hardly anyone is genuinely modest; their modesty is a front designed to elicit even more compliments.

People are, he thinks, largely motivated by *amour-propre* – that is, the desire to think well of themselves. This selfish motive lies behind much of what, on the surface, looks like virtuous or kind behaviour.

An odd but revealing fact is that La Rochefoucauld was not bitter or mean in his personal conduct; he was famously warm, friendly, funny and gracious. For him the great lesson of cynical truth is that this isn't the end point of thinking, it's the starting point.

He doesn't go into the world expecting people to be lovely and good at heart. He anticipates the inevitable, normal murkiness of human motives: the darker aspects are already factored in. He can then be pleasantly surprised and enchanted when someone turns out to be comparatively generous, thoughtful, forgiving or sweet-natured. As true Rochefoucauldian cynics we are easily pleased and hard to disappoint since – having carefully studied the human animal – we know what to expect.

Silvestro Valeri, *Portrait of Stendhal*,
1835–1836

*Why falling in love and staying in love
are so radically different.*

Stendhal,
On Love, 1822

One of the recurrent distresses of life is the frustration we are liable to feel around romantic love. We fall for someone but then get disappointed. Our love for them, we feel, has died. We move on and repeat the sorry scenario. We seem to find love but we can't keep it.

Stendhal is sympathetic to our suffering, which he knew well himself, and he offers a beautiful idea that may help us.

Born Marie-Henri Beyle (Stendhal was a pet name he devised for himself) in 1783, he had a respectable albeit dreary upbringing, but he began to flourish when, in his 20s, he became an administrator on the fringes of Napoleon's entourage. Later he served as French consul in a string of Italian cities. Somewhat corpulent in middle age, he was always keen on dressing well. Socially, he could be delightful – frank, warm and playful – but at parties he occasionally got irritated when the conversation struck him as superficial and conventional and he would become more and more outrageous – though he always regretted his outbursts afterwards.

De l'Amour (*On Love*) was first published in Paris in 1822, when he was nearing 40, though much of it was written in Milan in 1819 and 1820. Stendhal got the central idea for his book while he was holidaying in Salzburg. He went on a tour of a salt mine and was shown how a bare twig, left for a few days in the damp air, would become encrusted with salt crystals and become scintillating and beautiful.

This, he felt, is what happens when we fall in love: our minds encrust the other with delightful fantasies. We've enjoyed chatting to someone over various meals in restaurants and we imagine how lovely it would be to move into a dilapidated house and renovate it with them. They'd be enchanted by our ideas for interior decoration (just as they were enchanted with our choice of a Korean bar for drinks); they'll smile sweetly when we knock over the paint (just as they laughed sweetly when we accidentally dropped our butter knife). We take real things about them and grow huge daydreams around them. Of course, it is unlikely that anyone will be like this in reality. We get together and it turns out they are dismayed by our clumsiness and rather inflexible around decor. Hence the encounter with who the other person actually is feels like a process of disenchantment.

But, Stendhal says, *if* we realise that our picture of them was *always* a fantasy, we no longer expect them to live up to it and we're no longer so disheartened when, almost inevitably, they don't.

Stendhal performs a rescue operation on our love lives: in effect, he begs us not to confuse infatuation (delightful though it is) with long-term love. The two have very little in common. One is obsessed with the salt crystals, which have in fact come from our own imaginations; the other appreciates the real, though more modest, qualities of our actual twig-companion.

Sigmund Freud at his desk, Maresfield
Gardens, Hampstead, c. 1938

Freud's explosive work on erotic
experience was first published in 1905,
when Freud was in his early 50s.

Sigmund Freud,
Three Essays on the Theory of Sexuality, 1905

Broadly speaking, we seem to live in sexually open and enlightened times; our society as a whole is accepting, and even at times welcoming, of a wide variety of sexual experience. And we are always only a few clicks away from contact with erotic interests that would have startled (and horrified) earlier generations. But at an intimate level, our lives are often radically restricted: with a partner we may be ashamed or embarrassed to admit to our real enthusiasms. Even on our own we can be disturbed by the longings and fantasies that surge through our minds at moments of maximum excitement.

Born in 1856, Freud studied medicine in Vienna, where he came to specialise in psychiatry. His breakthrough – and the start of what was to become psychoanalysis – came when he began asking his distressed patients to tell him about their dreams and fantasies. It was an experience that would become familiar to therapists around the world: the most normal-looking client will, eventually, disclose bizarre-seeming secrets.

In his *Three Essays*, Freud explores the deep problem that our erotic curiosity inevitably starts in childhood: a period when, of course, caring adults must intently shield us from this entire topic. For powerfully important reasons, modern sexuality grows in the dark. Stray associations – a smell, certain items of clothing, particular words – become extremely important to us even though they have nothing to do with the biological purpose of sex, which is simply reproduction. What might (with no harsh judge-ment implied) be called 'perversion' is a natural, unavoidable result.

Freud suggests that 'normality' isn't par-ticularly normal. Our erotic preoccupations may feel odd (and we may be reluctant to admit them to others), but they are always un-derstandable and surprisingly widespread.

In modern life we have to feel, Freud argues, that sex is bad because it is opposed to so many other things we care about. It truly is bizarre: someone who is generally very interested in gaining status finds they are erotically excited by humiliation; someone who is committed to gentleness everywhere else in their life has fantasies of dominating others or of being dominated. It's as if our erotic minds don't listen to the rest of what our brains are saying. We may be committed to monogamy yet find ourselves excited by wild notions of anonymous encounters; we may be outwardly shy but secretly longing to flaunt ourselves in public.

Freud's kindness is to make this less disconcerting. It's not actually strange, he says, that we have these larger sexual dimensions. We needn't always act on them, but it makes sense that we have them. Our reasonable and important commitment to being good people comes into conflict with the subterranean origins of our erotic imagination. Perhaps we'll never, in our lives, tell anyone what it's really like to be us, but in the company of his book we can feel we're in the company of someone who would be willing and ready to hear the whole story.

Richmal Crompton, *Just William's Luck*,
1948

*Dishevelled, always getting into trouble,
never tidies his room — William may be
one of the role models we need.*

Richmal Crompton,
Just William, 1922–1970

It might sound odd, but a childhood can go deeply wrong if we are too concerned about being good.

On the surface, a 'good child' seems ideal: they are polite, reliable, cheerful, focused on schoolwork; they willingly help around the house and keep their room tidy. The problem below the surface is why they are like this. It is not because they are magically endowed with ideal qualities but because they are anxiously attuned to do what is wanted. They seek to please adults because they are terrified of what might happen if someone becomes upset.

William Brown, the schoolboy hero of Richmal Crompton's long-running series, is compelling and useful because he's superficially very different from the 'good child': he's messy, noisy, sceptical of school, argumentative and essentially untroubled about what others think of him.

However, William is a compelling and entertaining character because he is not malicious. His motto is: 'doin' good and rightin' wrongs'. His determination to be loyal to what he thinks is genuinely important leads him to behave in ways that, to conventional eyes, look wild and careless. He doesn't enjoy making grown-ups cross, but he's not afraid of their disapproval.

He doesn't see why having muddy knees is terrible while having a banal conversation in the drawing room is meant to be admirable; why is mastery of French verbs approved of while teaching your dog to dance is not?

William illustrates a slightly terrifying truth: to properly be ourselves, we may have to upset others. We may have to resign from a job, even though they will struggle to replace us, or tell someone that a relationship isn't working, even though they will take it badly. We will have to reject plans even though others want us to go through with them, because we have to prioritise other concerns. Often the mere thought of another's adverse reaction is enough to make us submit to something that we know we should step away from.

The overly good child becomes the painfully compliant adult. Richmal Crompton, via William, teaches us to like and admire the independent, less frightened, aspect of ourselves.

A funny thing about the *Just William* stories is that Crompton wrote them specifically for adults, although they became classics for generations of children – their elaborate vocabulary and complex sentence structure contravene perceived wisdom on how to address young readers. She wanted grown-ups to learn to like and appreciate their own inner, often neglected, William-ness. We are not difficult out of selfishness or weakness but because we are more bravely focused on what we truly believe in.

OVER 1,000,000 COPIES OF THIS BOOK HAVE BEEN SOLD
THE MOST POPULAR WORK OF NON-FICTION OF OUR TIME

HOW TO WIN FRIENDS AND INFLUENCE PEOPLE
BY DALE CARNEGIE

1. What are the six ways of making people like you? *See pages 75-133.*

2. What are the twelve ways of winning people to your way of thinking? *See pages 137-217.*

3. What are the nine ways to change people without giving offense 'or arousing resentment? *See pages 221-253.*

Dale Carnegie, *How to Win Friends and Influence People*, 1936

It's shocking how simple, obvious, yet urgently needed Carnegie's advice is.

Dale Carnegie,
How to Win Friends and Influence People, 1936

One of the terrors of modern life is that, while the truth may be known, it is ineffective; in democracies and markets, where numbers are decisive, it doesn't matter how wrong someone is, so long as they have enough supporters.

The world could be transformed if experts could win more friends and thus extend the range of their influence. The tragedy of the world is not so much that people in general are stupid (as, in irate moments, one might feel) but that not enough clever people have taken to heart Dale Carnegie's simple but eternal advice.

Born in 1888 into a poor farming family in rural Missouri, Carnegie left school in his teens. Rather than attend university, he spent years selling bacon and soap to people living on isolated ranches. He then got involved in adult education and spent thousands of evenings giving talks to small audiences in out-of-the-way towns. With prominent ears and a prosaic haircut, Dale Carnegie was almost the antitheses of what we imagine a great and centrally important writer might be like. In 1936, when he was in his late 40s, he summed up his views on being nice in a book that was ridiculed by intellectuals: *How to Win Friends and Influence People.*

The issues he addresses are basic: we spend vast parts of our lives trying to build relationships, hoping to get others to appreciate who we are, to understand us and grasp what we have to offer them, yet our efforts are often far from successful. Carnegie pinpointed things we desperately need to know and get good at but that had been largely neglected by previous writers.

What he suggests sounds like common sense: smile, remember someone's name, listen to them, think about what they want, don't make your success come at the price of theirs, don't tell others they are wrong, get to understand (and appreciate) why they think as they do, especially if it strikes you as misguided. And yet, these are precisely the things we generally forget to do. He recognised, with astonishing clarity, how naïve-sounding the advice we need really is.

Our culture wants us to imagine that what we need to know are very complicated things: a university will make sure its science students understand the theory of relativity or that its humanities graduates are acquainted with Foucault's views on 19th-century prisons. We're quite good at abstruse things. And yet we trip up on issues that are diametrically opposite in character; that are simple, emotional, interpersonal. They involve not demonstrating how much we know but rather showing how much we can like other people.

Knowledge of the truth is a tiny fraction of what it takes to make truth effective in the world. We are persuaded to change our minds only by people we like and who we feel love and understand us; that is, by people who have taken Carnegie's lessons to heart.

Anna Freud at her desk in Berggasse 19,
Vienna, c. 1920. Anna was the youngest
daughter of Sigmund Freud and the founder
of child psychoanalysis.

*We don't, of course, think of ourselves
as 'defensive', though we might be
tempted to apply this unlovely label
to others.*

Anna Freud,
The Ego and the Mechanisms of Defence, 1936

We offer a very just criticism; our friend or partner rejects it out of hand. We make an intelligent suggestion about an option; we're shouted down. Even our words of praise can meet with a blank refusal. Why are others sometimes so difficult? (Of course, others may ask the same question about us.)

The point of a defence mechanism, as Anna Freud beautifully explains, is that it is designed to stop us recognising something that actually is troubling us deeply. It stops us having to notice what's going wrong, though the underlying trouble always catches up with us.

Born in Vienna, in 1895, Anna was the sixth, and youngest, child of Sigmund Freud, the founder of psychoanalysis. She wrote *The Ego and the Mechanisms of Defence* in Vienna in 1936, as the political situation in Europe was rapidly degenerating. It was a horrendous time but one in which the desire to protect oneself from unwelcome news was perhaps especially apparent.

A classic 'defence' is *denial*. In denial we pretend to ourselves all is well. If someone tells us we're being reckless with money or drinking too much, or that the Nazis are coming to power, we brush aside their remarks: we 'know' everything is OK.

We do this, Anna Freud explains, not because we are stupid but because we're trying to protect our 'ego': our picture of who we are and how our life is going. We don't easily accept that we are harming ourselves or that others wish to harm us.

But this is only to touch the surface of how we might seek – sometimes at a terrible cost – to maintain a comfortable picture of who we are. When things go wrong, we find it tempting to blame others. They have let us down: we are innocent, just unfortunate. A price we pay for this comforting story is that we never investigate what we ourselves could do to improve our situation. We defend ourselves by aggression and explode at the person who nearly punctures our bubble. Or we regress: we are too weak, too sad and too hopeless to bear criticism, so they must stop. Or we see hostility everywhere in order to distract ourselves from our own unkind and brutish thoughts: we have been wronged by the universe, therefore we are licensed to unleash our rage and think well of ourselves at the same time. Or we become fantastically conciliatory: we apologise so very well, surely, after our eloquent outpourings, that no one can ask us to actually change our behaviour.

The key point, though, is that Anna Freud isn't blaming *us* for being defensive. As she sees it this is entirely natural, if unfortunate. What's amazing and wonderful and rare is that we ever get interested in trying to deconstruct our psychic defences, embrace the more awkward truths and seek to live outside our protective shell. She's not criticising us for not doing this, she's tentatively offering to help us undertake this difficult but potentially exciting and life-transforming step.

Edouard de Pomiane, *Cooking in Ten Minutes*, cover of edition published in 1957

Our lives are often bedevilled by a well-meaning but stifling, and ultimately erroneous, idea of 'how things are meant to be done'.

Edouard de Pomiane,
Cooking in Ten Minutes, 1930

We can't write a book because we don't have two free years to labour on it. We can't take up dancing because we're too old. Or, as de Pomiane would easily imagine, we can't invite people round to dinner because we can't cook. Few topics are of more weight in our lives than that of self-confidence: we shy away from approaching the people we'd really like to be friends with; we put our life on hold because we can't face a particular administrative task; we limit who we are because we think so many things are beyond our capacity.

De Pomaine's beautiful strategy is to cut corners and find the simplest possible way of doing what we really want to. His recipes are absurdly easy. One 'recipe' for dessert is to buy chocolate eclairs on the way home. All the 'cooking' this requires is that we find a pretty plate to put them on. In the same spirit, he 'teaches' us how to buy ready-opened oysters and a lemon or how to open a tin of peas and 'add a curl of butter'. Tinned tuna mixed with mayonnaise from the supermarket is a treat.

It's especially nice to hear this message from him. Born in Paris in 1875 to parents who fled an anti-Semitic purge in Poland, he trained as a medical doctor and then worked as a research scientist at the Institut Pasteur, focusing on food preparation. He was a great gourmand. He's secure enough to know that such expertise is, in the end, a sideshow. His great underlying concern is that we should enjoy our meals with others: if we minimise preparation, if we trust his bare-bones suggestions, we can do something wonderful. We can sip wine with our friends, chat over coffee, listen (as he sweetly recommends) to a rumba playing on the gramophone. We shouldn't miss all this because we are worried we can't cook.

To certain people who know only the title, *La cuisine en dix minutes (Cooking in Ten Minutes)* might sound like just one more cynical money-spinner, promising something it can't deliver. Intriguingly, though, it was originally published, in 1930, by Editions Paul Matrial, a Parisian editorial house specialising in avant-garde art books. Nearly two decades later, it was released in English by Bruno Cassirer, the most highly cultivated and intellectual publisher of the time. The book is simple but written for sophisticated people.

The glory of the book is the way it invites us to imaginatively extend it. We can get the key thing – enjoyment – even if we are not much good at something. We can learn two dance moves that will see us through. We'll never be great, but that wasn't really the goal: we'll just have fun whirling with our friends. We don't have to be wise or learned: we just send a warm message that we'd like to receive, because almost everyone will like that too.

We are closer than we had dared to think to being able to do the things we've longed to but have, so sadly and unnecessarily, put off.

Merze Tate with her bike at Oxford
University, c. 1932

Why we need to respect our enemies –
especially when they are in the wrong.

Merze Tate,
The Disarmament Illusion, 1942

'Disarmament' is a poignant word. We know, whether politically or intimately in a relationship, that nothing is sweeter or more of a relief than for both sides to lay down their arms. Yet we have struggled collectively and individually to bring this about.

If I stop attacking you, will you stop threatening me? If I put down my emotional rifle, will you lower your psychological defences? If my country disarms so that we can put our resources into more constructive and desperately needed things, can I count on your country to do the same?

The moral logic is clear; peace is obviously what we want. Yet in practice, war is frequent. Why is it so hard for us to lay down our weapons? This is the problem Merze Tate wanted to solve.

Tate had a difficult path through higher education. Born in 1905 in rural Michigan, she was initially denied a university place. She taught in a small school, she attended night classes, she did a correspondence degree and eventually, in 1932 – just as Hitler came to power in Germany – she became the first African American woman to enrol for a master's degree at Oxford. There she studied international relations, before going on to gain a doctoral degree from Harvard.

Tate's specialist subject, on which she wrote her great book, was the failure of the many disarmament initiatives of the late 19th and early 20th centuries. They had been intellectually sophisticated and well intentioned but had culminated in the horrors of World War I. Researching and writing the book from 1933 to 1940, Tate was staring directly at the next horrific failure of the noble longing for peace.

Tate's great thesis is that we have to make a clear distinction between morality and what she calls 'politics': simply, the reality of how others happen to view their interests, whether justified or not.

In the end, Tate thinks, the grave cause of conflict is humiliation. A humiliated nation – or person – does not want to disarm; they desperately want to become strong enough to exact revenge. The path to peace, therefore, is to recognise the dignity of the other, on their terms. This is hard because their conception of their honour may be entirely at odds with our vision of what it should be. The price of peace, Tate argues, is that we allow the other to be 'wrong' as we see it.

It is only those who feel respected who can afford to disarm. This is what so many peace plans got wrong. They didn't properly recognise how hurt others might feel, even if irrationally.

Tate says that peace comes when we stop trying to be right. We have to grant equality even to our enemies before we can ask them to trust us.

Ingrid Vang Nyman, illustration of
Pippi Longstocking

We spend too much of our lives concerned
about what others think of us.

Astrid Lindgren,
Pippi Longstocking, 1945

Being concerned about what others think of us is a very understandable preoccupation. We evolved as social animals, required to maintain our place within our tribal group, on which the necessities of existence depended. But this mentality can lead us to massively over-estimate how much, now, such approval actually matters.

First published in Swedish in 1945, and perfectly illustrated by Ingrid Vang Nyman, the book had its origins in 1941. As World War II was grimly unfolding and the Germans were invading Russia, Astrid Lindgren was living in Stockholm. One evening, her anxious young daughter, Karin, asked her to tell her a story.

Lindgren herself wasn't daunted by convention. Born in 1907, she grew up in a characteristically elegant small town in the south of Sweden. After school, she got a job as a journalist, became involved with the editor, got pregnant and went to Denmark to give birth. Soon after she moved to Stockholm, in Sweden, and became involved in the burgeoning sport of motor racing (she was one of the organisers of the 1933 Swedish Grand Prix). She eventually married the head of the Swedish Royal Automobile Club and made a great deal of money from her books, but lived the remainder of her long life in a modest flat in the centre of the city. When she died in her 90s, she was a national hero, and her supposedly scandalous behaviour (as it must have seemed at the time) turned out not to have mattered at all.

The Pippi that she imagined in response to her daughter's request is a 9-year-old girl with strikingly red hair and masses of freckles – a very conspicuous appearance for a young Swedish girl of the time. She's spent most of her life at sea with her father, a ship's captain. But her father has somehow gone missing in the South Pacific – no doubt he's fine, just out of reach. So Pippi turns up in a small town with a suitcase full of gold coins, a pet monkey (known as Mr Nilsson) and a nameless horse, which, wonderfully, she can lift off the ground with one hand. She proceeds to occupy a charming, rather large villa and sets about making friends with a couple of local children.

It's strange, in a way: Pippi isn't obviously likeable. She doesn't bother if she upsets the occasional person; she isn't remotely apologetic for her actions; she delights in her own merits and generally thinks she's pretty much perfect in every way. No one could be less conventional than Pippi and yet she is one of the most beloved characters in the history of books for children.

We fear people won't respect us, yet what people so often want is to find the suppressed, adventurous, independent part of themselves advocated by another.

A drawing of Melanie Klein by one of
her child patients, 1926

Why is it so hard to accept complexity
in ourselves and others?

Melanie Klein,
Envy and Gratitude and Other Works 1946–1963,
1957

What can technically be called polarisation is one of the scourges of relationships and of collective life. Many people seem compelled to see themselves as wholly good and 'the other' as wholly bad. The obviously sane view that we are all a subtle mixture of flaws and virtues is remarkably hard to sustain in practice. This is a tendency in human nature that massively increases conflict and makes workable solutions much harder to find. Tragically, the feeling that *I am right and you are wrong* is one of the most enticing and satisfying (however unjust) of human passions.

Perhaps the most illuminating writer on why we avoid nuance was the Jewish psychoanalyst Melanie Klein. Born in Vienna in 1882, she relocated, in her mid-40s, to London, where she died in 1960. She was one of the first people to be devoted to the study of the emotional development of young children.

Klein observed that babies unavoidably split their feelings into two opposed camps. When things are going well, everyone is good. But when they get frustrated, or are in pain, everyone is bad: an infant suffering from indigestion feels that the entire world is horrible.

Melanie Klein's generous point is that this is where we inevitably start. *Of course* we begin with starkly opposed categories: the wholly good and the entirely awful. The difficult thing isn't to explain how we fall into a polarised view of the world, but rather to understand what can help us find a way out.

It's a sign, perhaps, of how unready we are collectively to dismantle our own black-and-white thinking that Melanie Klein's essays weren't widely published until 1975, some fifteen years after her death.

Klein's core contention is that we need to shift perspective and think about 'grown-ups' as they really are. To a growing child, a parent is first a god and then a massive disappointment.

It's almost impossible for a 4-year-old to imagine that a parent might be justifiably preoccupied; that they might be late not because they don't care but because they are under a lot of pressure; that they recall being little and empathise with us even if they can't always do what we want; that they love us more than words can say and will, unavoidably, mess up our lives.

A person can try sincerely and fail; they can be utterly wrong for understandable reasons; they can mean well and mess up; they can love us and end up letting us down. But we're not simply grasping these painful facts about others, we're having to accept them as truths about ourselves.

Maturity begins when we realise and can gracefully accept the impurity of everything.

Mark Gerson, *Donald Winnicott*, July 1963

*We try too hard to be good, when the real
task is to be ourselves.*

Donald Winnicott,
Home Is Where We Start From, 1990

A key focus of Winnicott's concern, one that can reach deeply into our own lives, is the danger of being 'too good'. On the surface it's a strange worry. Surely the better we can be, the better? But he grasped how it is a feeling of inadequacy, a kind of desperation, that impels us – at a sometimes high cost – to excel, to be perfect, to win, to triumph and to overawe others with our splendid achievements.

Donald Winnicott was born in Plymouth, a city on the south coast of England, in 1896. His father was prominent in business, becoming mayor and earning a knighthood; his mother, though sweet-natured, was often depressed. As a child, Winnicott came to think that his function in life was to cheer her up, make her proud of him and generally be the ideal child.

His great good fortune, as he saw it, was to become a difficult, rebellious teenager. He later studied medicine and qualified as a psychoanalyst – the first senior psychiatrist in the UK to do so. Unusually, even as he attained professional eminence, he retained a great sympathy and fondness for his younger naughty, even delinquent, self.

The essays that make up this book were first published in 1986, by the US publisher W.W. Norton and Co, fifteen years after Winnicott's death. They were papers he didn't quite have the confidence to finish or make public, perhaps still struggling with what his mother would have made of them.

As a medical practitioner, Winnicott could assert that 'health is tolerant of ill health': a healthy person isn't someone who is never exposed to germs or illness, but rather one who, when confronted by disease, can cope; their body is invaded but they are good at recovery. The healthy person, therefore, isn't easily terrified of infection or disease. They sense they are robust enough to cope with the ordinary threats; they'll get the flu but they'll be OK; they'll come down with a cold but soon get better.

What really interested him was the psychological version of this sense of resilience: of course I'll mess up, but I can have another go; yes, I let someone down, but I can do better next time; I'm a total idiot in a couple of directions, but pretty sensible and competent about a lot of other things. If we hold ourselves rigidly to perfection, we can't make these healthy accommodations – every mistake feels like the end of the world.

This applies in our duties to others. No parent can be perfect, but that might not matter. They are showing their child how to recover, how to apologise, how to offer to make things right after a failing, how – in the psychological sense – to be more robust.

We don't need to be perfect. We only need, as Winnicott beautifully puts it, to be 'good enough' – that is, to be flexible enough to cope with the failings and troubles that unavoidably come our way.

Onjali Raúf, *The Boy at the Back of the Class*, 2018

Reconnecting ourselves with the more trusting, less cynical, parts of who we used to be.

Onjali Raúf,
The Boy at the Back of the Class, 2018

Many people today find it absurd to believe in, or admire, the monarchy. How could a sane adult wish there to be someone who stands above democracy? How could you wish there to be a power above you? How could you admire an institution not directly answerable to the will of the people?

In a school in London, we meet a new boy, Ahmet, who sits at the back and won't look at, let alone speak to, anyone. Some of his class-mates regard him with suspicion, but a few are interested in getting to know him.

What they discover, as they gradually become friends – alongside the fact that Ahmet is skilled at football – is that he is caught up in a tragedy of the wider world: he's a refugee from Syria and has become separated from his father.

The book is beautifully written for 8 to 10 year-olds. But how can Ahmet's new friends help him? How can children get things done in the adult world? To whom can they possibly turn?

The children hit upon a plan that only exists in books, yet one that tells us so much. In a daring escapade, they appeal to the Queen of England. They imagine she can surely help.

Of course, as British adults know, a British monarch has no executive power. But the beauty of the book is that it doesn't belittle the children's hopes. The Queen herself can do nothing, but her security detail can reach out to their friends, and eventually Ahmet's father is found and brought safely to London.

This is not, of course, a documentary-style book: it speaks to longings rather than to factual likelihood. Via the persona of the Queen, its theme is that of the benign adult; the good parent.

At times, we are the boy at the back of the class: we need to ask for help, but we cannot. We wish we could turn to a greater and kinder authority; to someone wearing a crown who could understand our needs without having to worry whether this would be approved by col-leagues or constituencies or, indeed, by the country at large. We long for there to be someone in the highest position who could understand.

As adults we need to read books written for children. They reconnect us with parts of ourselves that, in later life, we tend to disdain: trusting, noble and ready to admire authority so long as it comes in a kindly guise – and a golden coach.

VI.
Memoirs

Katsushika Hokusai, *Young Woman Reading
'The Pillow Book (Makura no Sōshi)'*, 1822

*What makes a life fascinating isn't the
dramatic events that occur but the way we
think and feel about ordinary things.*

Sei Shonagon,
The Pillow Book, 1002

At times it feels natural to lament how boring our lives are. We do the same sorts of things each week; nothing special or exciting ever seems to happen. We enviously compare our dull routines to the adventures of others.

An antidote to our sense of tedium can be found in the work of Sei Shonagon. Around a thousand years ago, she kept a journal of the decade or so she spent as a lady-in-waiting at the Imperial Palace in Kyoto, then the capital of Japan. Despite the high status of her job, her daily life was, externally, uneventful: an afternoon's carriage ride outside the walls of the court compound might be the highlight of a year; a day trip to hear a sermon in a temple seems to have been the farthest extent of her travels; she spent almost all of her time indoors, in just two or three rooms; she saw the same few people month after month; her work largely involved keeping respectfully silent, knowing when to bow and remembering the complex titles of various officials.

Yet *Makura no Sōshi* (*The Pillow Book*) gives the impression that she had a wonderful time. We don't really know where the lovely title of the book came from; perhaps she slept with it under her head, occasionally adding a thought or observation by the light of the moon.

Typically she asks herself questions, for instance: what is the nicest time of day? In the summer it's the night, especially if it's raining; in spring she prefers the dawn; in autumn, sunset; in winter, the morning. An 'event' in her day includes observing the frost on the branches of a plum tree or enjoying the beating of the rain on the veranda roof. Such things don't sound very thrilling, but by concentrating on them and appreciating them, they become deep sources of satisfaction.

Or she might ask herself: what is it fun to see? It might be someone who is usually very formal in their dress turning up looking dishevelled; a curtain at an open window billowing in the breeze; a cat walking easily along the top of a narrow railing; water droplets on leaves in the garden; porters cleverly manoeuvring a big load that one would think would be impossibly cumbersome to carry; people whose clothes match the colour of the room they are in.

She makes lists of words that sound intriguing, and of place names that sound romantic. She delights in describing little things that annoy her: someone who takes too long telling a good story; something clever she could have said but didn't think of at the time; trying to get something done too quickly, making a mess of it and having to start all over again.

As we read, we might wish our life were as interesting as hers, yet she secretly shares the technique that would make our own existence equally rich if we knew to ask ourselves more interesting questions. As with so many great books, it leaves us not so much wanting to read it again as to start writing our own private version.

Wittgenstein's cabin rebuilt in
Sognefjord, near Skjolden, Norway, 2019

*We desperately fear poverty –
but should we?*

Chomei,
The Ten Foot Square Hut, 1212

One of the deep, haunting worries of life is that, with a downturn of luck, or due to some stupid mistake of our own, we may conspicuously fail in economic terms. We'll lose, or will never acquire, an elegant house in a good area; we'll not be able to afford to eat in fine restaurants or travel in style. We're not talking about poverty in general but only about the special case of those who have known comfort and even wealth and who are terrified of losing it.

Here Chomei is our sweetest friend. He himself had come down badly in the world. He was born some time in the 1150s and grew up in the family mansion. His father was in charge of a major religious shrine in the imperial city of Kyoto. Chomei expected an equally prestigious and lucrative career but struggled to find recognition as a poet or a musician. He held (in his own eyes and those of his elegant friends) lowly, low-paid posts; he mismanaged his dwindling resources. At 50, in shame and despair, he gave up and retreated to a monastery, but he failed even there. Finally, he went to live in the woods, in a tiny hut he built himself. Life there was extremely basic: plumbing was merely a nearby stream; he had to cook outdoors (eventually he added a small veranda to keep off the rain); he owned only three books; his bed was made of bracken he collected in the forest.

What starts to emerge, however, is that he was happier here – in this forsaken, impoverished (as his former friends would see it) existence: 'I can rest and laze as I wish, there is no one to stand in my way or shame me.'

He liked playing the *biwa*, the medieval Japanese equivalent of the guitar: 'My skill is poor, but then I do not aim to please the ears of others. I play alone, I sing alone, simply for my own fulfilment.'

He spent time contemplating the distant view to the sea; he liked the sound of rain falling through the trees. On rare occasions he visited the city: 'There I am ashamed of my low, beggarly status, but once back here again I pity those who chase after the sordid rewards of the world.'

It was in his tiny hut that he found the inner freedom to write his best work. Failure, he came to think, is actually the norm. All success is temporary; apparent success is accompanied by anxiety and has to be defended against envy.

He discovered – as we too might, *in extremis* – that he no longer missed what he used to have. He could get by with very little; the successes of others did not torment him and he no longer cared what others might, or might not, make of him.

What the world calls failure could turn out to be fine. We may never have to put this to the test, but spending time with Chomei lessens our fear that we might.

Frederick Douglass in his Cedar Hill
library, c. 1885

*We have no idea how our lives will change
in ten or twenty years.*

Frederick Douglass,
The Life and Times of Frederick Douglass,
1881

It's difficult for us to comprehend the changes that time inevitably brings, though we've had endless lessons in it. At 5 we had no picture of being 15; at 15 our vision of 25 was wildly wrong; between 25 and 45 we become, perhaps, the opposite of what we'd anticipated. Yet we find it so hard to learn: we keep on imagining that *now* we know what our future will be like.

Frederick Douglass was born into slavery in the US state of Maryland in 1817. As a child he was separated from his mother; his father was rumoured to have been a white slave owner. Our instinct is to read the life of Frederick Douglass simply as an indictment of slavery, though it's unlikely that we need persuasion on this point. His memoir, perhaps, is more to be honoured for being universal: it teaches us that we cannot begin to see in advance the unfolding of our lives.

In his early teens, Douglass was hired out by his owner to a comparatively benign master in Baltimore; on errands in the city he taught himself to read and started teaching other slaves on Sundays. At 20 he met and fell in love with a freeborn black woman, Anna Murray. She plotted his route to freedom. The following year, disguised as a sailor and carrying false identification papers, he made his way to New York, where local slave ownership had been abolished (though fugitives from elsewhere were still required to be returned to servitude). He found refuge in the house of a prominent black journalist. Anna joined him, they married and he was ordained as a preacher.

Still in his 20s, Douglass was recruited in a major political drive. He lectured in many states and was heard by large audiences, though he was also insulted and menaced in the streets. He travelled to the UK where, on his first evening, he was astonished to be invited to a grand restaurant where no one objected to his presence. In London, well-wishers purchased his freedom and set him up with capital to launch a newspaper back in the USA. Under a universalist motto – 'Rights have no sex, truth has no colour' – it was a significant success. He wrote his memoirs, which became a bestseller; he bought a large villa surrounded by a beautiful garden; he became the friend of presidents, asserting that he 'would work with anyone to do good'.

Towards the very end of his life (he died in 1895) he contacted the most brutal owner of his youth. Citing the Christian idea of 'love the sinner, hate the sin', he forgave the wrongs done to him and sought and found reconciliation with the monster who had treated him so cruelly.

When he was born it couldn't possibly have been predicted how his life would turn out or what he would become. His life, surely, contains more tragedy and more success than our own, but it speaks to a fundamental and hopeful theme: the unknowability of the future.

THE AUTHOR.

Frontispiece.

Elizabeth Grant Smith, *Memoirs of a Highland lady; the autobiography of Elizabeth Grant of Rothiemurchus, afterwards Mrs. Smith of Baltiboys, 1797–1830*, frontispiece from edition published in 1911

Who deserves empathy?

Elizabeth Grant,
Memoirs of a Highland Lady, 1898

As sensitive, serious people in the modern world, we are very concerned about empathy. Our kindness and imagination readily enter into the lives of the obviously distressed. So many people have a much harder time than we do and our hearts go out to them. There's a curious consequence of our kindness: we are empathy givers, not empathy receivers. If we are statistically fortunate, empathy is always portrayed as downward directed; no one can feel *for us*.

Yet we may need tender understanding. Our troubles are intensely real to us, yet there's a psychological block: we find it hard to view our situation with warm generosity. We deserve blame, not forgiving insight.

Elizabeth Grant is a useful companion in this respect because she was, in many ways, immensely lucky. She was born in one of the most beautiful houses in Edinburgh in 1797 into a great landowning Scottish family. She started writing the story of her life when she was in her 40s, imagining the material would only ever be read by her family circle. An abridged version was made public in 1898, more than a decade after her death; the full text was only published in the early years of the 21st century.

She had her sorrows and her sufferings, although the things she had to struggle with wouldn't, today, much touch the souls of many well-meaning people. When her father lost a great deal of money in her late teens, they had to move to India, where he was given a high-ranking official post. Grant faced this humiliation with immense bravery and good humour – but who will sympathise? What to her felt like a terrible climbdown was to the rest of the world a cynical shuffling of privilege.

Later, when she married, she moved to Ireland to live on her husband's landed estate. She had endless anxieties: the roof of the mansion was in a poor state and they didn't have the money to restore it. She worried greatly about the condition of their tenant farmers, though there was little she could do to improve their lives. She was always anxious her sons might not have the wealth necessary to maintain their station in life. Officially, she's unworthy of a moment's sympathy. Yet her memoirs show she's obviously a delightful person; she's warm, funny, generous, down to earth and loving.

To open our hearts to her is an education because – metaphorically – she is us. We may not live in a mansion, but in global and historical terms we too are very fortunate. To feel a loving sympathy towards Elizabeth Grant is to do a profound thing: it is to recognise that everyone's sorrows, fears and terrors are legitimate, including our own.

Self-directed empathy means internalising the kindness we readily offer others. Being brutal towards ourselves doesn't make us better people; we become sweeter to others when we're sweeter to ourselves. It's not special pleading: we're allowing ourselves to be treated equally; empathy points in all directions, including directly into our own hearts.

E.O. Hoppé, *Halide Edib Adivar*, 1927

*The true, inside story of nearly every
life, told in detail, sounds absurd.*

Halide Edib,
The Memoirs, 1926

There is, perhaps, no weirder or more rewarding undertaking than to tell the story of our own lives. It's so hard because we are continually buffeted by internalised assumptions about who we are supposed to be and what we are meant to feel. We lose touch with the fact that we grew up immersed in a particular environment that to us was the whole world, and we had no idea of what could possibly occur in our lives.

No one can plausibly be blamed for their childhood, yet it cannot help but influence our later outlook and attitudes. We can be very cruel to ourselves when we judge what we were like when we were little by the standards of what we now believe.

In her autobiography, Halide Edib is deeply compassionate to her childhood self. Born into the upper echelons of the rapidly decaying Ottoman Empire, she took it for granted growing up that her grandmother might have occult powers; that she couldn't go into the garden unless accompanied by a male servant; that her loving father should have two legal wives; that her relatives should occupy the highest positions of power; that she should rest in the shade while others worked.

Our modern, egalitarian and rational assumptions are supposed to bridle at such admissions. But this truly was her experience. She couldn't forget the run-down beauty of the huge house overlooking the Bosporus or the loving fidelity of the servants.

Edib grew up to realise that the world of her childhood would not be the world of the future. She became a controversial figure: a nationalist politician who would do anything (including perhaps some terrible things) to support the cause of the new state of Turkiye that was emerging from the ruins of the old empire. She could be seen as either a heroine or a monster, as we all can be, if only in lesser terms. For all of us, there is the heroic version of our lives and the equally (if not more) compelling tally of our errors and regrets.

The magic of Edib is that she allows the innocence of her childhood to survive. She can always reconnect with the existential questions that she first encountered on looking in a mirror around the age of 6: *why is this me? Might I not be, or have been, someone else? Why should these be my eyes or this my hair? Why should these things define me?*

Her inspiration is that we might do the same. We will always fail to be the adults we should ideally be, but we will never stop being the children we actually were. So we can, with honour, tell the complex, perhaps unacceptable, but very real story of how we ended up as who we are.

Malcolm X reading stories about himself
in a pile of newspapers, c. 1963

Maybe the answer is divorce.

Malcolm X,
The Autobiography of Malcolm X, 1965

One of the instincts of many decent people is to feel that we have to make peace with our enemies: we have to find a way of living together. It can show up, historically, as appeasement – that is, as the search for a way of placating and soothing the demands of an aggressor; or, more intimately, as the long and perhaps fruitless search for a way of coordinating our own needs and desires with those of a partner.

It's this instinct that Malcolm X resoundingly and inspiringly rejects. He was drawn to the virtues of refusal and the merits of separation.

Born Malcolm Little in 1925, his father died when he was young and his mother was often under psychiatric care. In his teens he drifted into a criminal underworld and from his early 20s he was imprisoned for seven years. While incarcerated he devoted himself to reading, studied philosophy and converted to Islam; he also changed his name to X, to signal his forced ignorance of his true heritage. Released in 1952, he joined a radical Chicago-based faith group, the Nation of Islam, and quickly rose to prominence as their leading political orator. He came to think that black and white America should, in effect, break up. There was no point in seeking justice for the wrongs of slavery and oppression; he didn't think that the guarantee of a few legal rights or even a financial settlement could bring real justice. Maybe the USA should be divided into two distinct countries, or maybe the black population should leave; in any case, the solution was a complete break.

In his late 30s, Malcolm X began to write his autobiography, collaborating with the prominent African American journalist Alex Haley. While writing the book he decided to break with the Nation of Islam. This was viewed as a betrayal, and in February 1965 he was assassinated by members of the group. The book came out eight months later.

Malcolm X was, of course, a major figure in US racial politics, but the deepest emotional message of his work is, perhaps, distinct from the time and place in which he lived. Essentially, he says that certain problems can't be solved by compromise. We may, by chance, have been born in a place that really is disastrous for us. Rather than forcing ourselves to recognise its (limited) merits and fit in with its traditions, maybe we should just leave. If a relationship has been agonising for months or years, maybe the problem isn't that we are inflexible but just that it's wrong for us. Malcolm X dignifies our struggle. He's the voice that says, yes, you may be able to extract a little change here or there, but this will never bring you real freedom. We have to, he says, take up arms. The other (be it a country or a person) will never love us but will keep on making claims on us. We have to fight our way out.

Intermezzo:
A Note on Titles

Benedict Anderson, *Imagined Communities*,
cover of edition published in 1983

*We yearn to belong, but is there any
actual society where we truly do?*

Benedict Anderson,
Imagined Communities, 1983

In principle, we might want to be part of a tribe or a clan. We would love to feel that we fit in, that our personal values are shared by many, that we are appreciated and that our efforts contribute effectively to the collective good. But often this generous impulse to join in is thwarted: we can't actually find the community we need.

Benedict Anderson was born in 1936 in China to upper-class Irish parents. He studied in England, became a professor at Cornell University in New York and spent many years living in Indonesia, Vietnam and Cambodia. He was fluent in more than a dozen languages. He was a representative of the modern spirit: living outside a traditional community yet fascinated by the idea of belonging.

In *Imagined Communities*, published in 1983, Anderson explores the emergence of nationalism in the 19th century. Traditionally, communities have been founded on external, physical factors: blood relatives, a feeling of loyalty to the people who happen to dwell in the same village or valley or perhaps city. Nationalism, as Anderson sees it, was invented by political leaders as a way to unite many such disparate groups. Flags, myths, anthems and ideas about the land and ethnicity were deployed to generate intense feelings of collective identity – and to foment collective hostility. A united 'people' could then be motivated to fight for independence or self-government. It was a potent move, but in Anderson's analysis, it didn't properly serve the true interests of the population. A new nation detaches itself from its imperial overlords, but that doesn't mean that the 'liberated' country will automatically have a more just economy or wiser laws or more kindly or generous attitudes.

But the fascination of the book isn't specifically to do with its intelligent doubts about the phenomenon of national identity. Instead it's to do with the wider possibilities around imagined communities that we can elaborate for ourselves.

There have been fascinating examples of group identity: revolutionary communist cells, intense religious societies, scientific teams collaborating on a vast project, a band of adventurers trying to make it to the South Pole. It's appealing that they've come together because they share an idea – even when, sadly, it's not an idea we ourselves feel enthusiastic about.

Yet the ideas-based imaginative community we long for may be more available to us than we suppose. Our 'nation' – in terms of emotions, values and mentality – is constituted by the artists, philosophers and writers we love. Such an imagined community is one central way of describing a therapeutic library; it's the forum, or meeting place, of the ideas we need around us for support, comfort and encouragement: our little group, our ideal tribe.

In our library we're not defined by our taste in clothes or our sexuality or where we were born or our job or who our parents are. What matters is what we find moving or inspiring, tender or beautiful. It's our secret selves that our books want to welcome and make friends with.

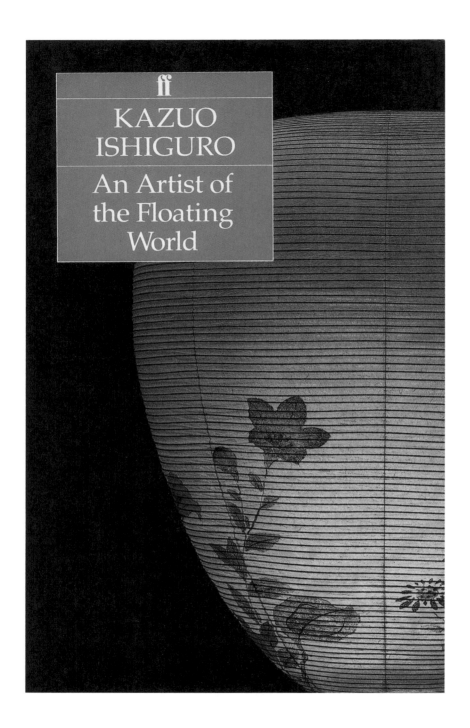

KAZUO ISHIGURO

An Artist of the Floating World

Kazuo Ishiguro, *An Artist of the Floating World*, cover of edition published in 1986

It's no act of disrespect: by not reading a book we keep its promise permanently open and alive.

Kazuo Ishiguro,
An Artist of the Floating World, 1986

It seems unfair to keep a book around us and never open its pages. Yet there may be a very good motive for doing so: we love the title so much that we need to keep it for ourselves.

In 1986, the globally acclaimed novelist Kazuo Ishiguro brought out a book with what might be one of the most lovely titles of all time: *An Artist of the Floating World.* What is 'the floating world'? It might be the arena of daydreams and fantasies where ideas, half-formed plans and thoughts about what we could do are untethered from the constraints of reality: the places we think of visiting but never do; the life we could perhaps lead if we moved to the country or went to live on a small, sunny island; the businesses we think of setting up but never get round to; or what would happen if we did just go up and introduce ourselves to an interesting-looking stranger. A great deal of what happens in our imaginations doesn't happen in reality. In a stern mood, we could see all that as simply wasted thought. But perhaps the title suggests otherwise: perhaps it is saying that we cannot avoid having this vast hinterland of imaginative possibilities extending far out from the narrow course of what we actually do. Maybe it is inviting us to see ourselves as artists of this dimension of existence: the book could be encouraging us to appreciate these imagined sketches that we are always making and recognising them as important parts of who we are.

Or perhaps it is saying that we always have to live in the floating space between the past and the future; or that consciousness floats on top of the deeper, unconscious drives that shape our lives; or that we live in a world of uncertainties – yet it is a hopeful, calm and elegant title. It's not lamenting or panicking or complaining. It suggests, perhaps, that we can become skilled and refined in the way we deal with uncertainty or contingency.

Of course, it may not be about any of these things. We'll never know, because for us the great thing is to wonder what it *might* be about. If we opened a page, that fragile space of imagination would be replaced by empirical knowledge. Ishiguro, who won the Nobel Prize for Literature in 2017, is a writer of such eminent standing that our personal nonreading of one of his early works can hardly be seen as unkind.

The value of an unread book is that it is, as yet, all promise. We're not simply ignoring it: we'd ideally spent a lot of time actively, intensely, not reading it. It holds a prized position in our inner lives because it is the gateway not to the author's thoughts but to our own.

Gerhard Richter, *Grey*, 1974

*Sometimes what we really need from
a book — and its title — is a blank
screen onto which we can project our
own thoughts and feelings.*

Irina Ratushinskaya,
Grey Is the Colour of Hope, 1988

Without shame, we admit that this volume is among the many no-doubt-wonderful works of which we know only the title. In our crowded lives we can only give ourselves over to a few of the many things that, potentially, could speak powerfully to us. There are places we might love if we could visit them but that will remain simply intriguing names on a map. There are interesting faces we may see in the supermarket or at the airport, and if we got to know those people they might become friends, but we'll never know.

We need a philosophy of life that doesn't lament this or try to pretend that we have a duty to read every book, visit every place or talk to every interesting-looking stranger. Instead it would guiltlessly redirect our attention to the idea of *suggestiveness*. Instead of asking what X (a book, a place or a person) is really about or like, it asks: what we can imaginatively do, ourselves, with an intriguing hint?

It might make for an ideal exam question at a utopian school or university: *Answer this question only if you know more or less nothing about a book called* Grey Is the Colour of Hope: *outline what you'd love it to be about. (No marks are awarded for the chance correspondence of any of your suggestions to the actual contents of the work.)*

We trialled this question at the office on a busy Tuesday morning. Here are some of the answers:

1.   I'd love it to be about someone's reconciliation with the ageing process. As their hair fades they start to invest in the idea of maturity. They rebel against the tyrannical idea that it's better to be young. They keep doing those things we do when we're little (longing to be 18 or 21), but now they can't wait to be 60.

2.   The perfect thing would be a fun take on Hegel. He has this line where he says wisdom means 'painting grey in grey'. I reckon he means you get to be nuanced enough to appreciate the actual ambiguity of things; you stop pretending (or wanting) actually complicated stuff to be black or white. You start to like hearing people say: 'Well, it's tricky' or 'It's not that simple.' You see these as the voices of reason and hope.

3.   Please let it be a hymn to recovery: when you are cheery, hope feels obvious and bright; when you are really down even tiny things – the grey things – are what you hold on to. I brushed my teeth! I moved the bag of rubbish to near the door! I exercised for nine seconds! Pathetic? No, this is the little beginning of grey in the black night.

It's probably a work of genius. But sometimes the ideas we need are the ones we're trying to tell ourselves: we just need a little hint from another to get us going.

Earth over the horizon of the Moon,
taken during the Apollo 8 mission,
December 1968

When the outer world is in turmoil,
where can we find inner security?

Hilary Mantel,
A Place of Greater Safety, 1992

An intriguing title is pivotal. It's our chance to work out what we think; to write in our heads the outline of the book we'd ideally read.

We get so used to certain degrees of anxiety and fear that we stop wondering why our lives should be like this. A place of safety isn't so much a physical refuge as a psychological state in which we feel that whatever happens outside can't remove our basic self-worth.

There have been beguiling but not directly usable historical versions of this idea. An early Christian was 'safe' because even if they were persecuted, their soul had an eternal and glorious home in heaven.

Aristocrats later evolved a secular version of this: you could lose everything, but it was literally impossible to stop being the Marchioness of X or Sir So-and-so. The deepest basis of dignity, according to them, was untouchable by the tribulations of life.

From the late 19th century onwards, artists made a curious adaptation of this idea; a person might be totally unrecognised by the world, an individual economic disaster zone, but still be an artist. That was all that really mattered; the opinions of the public and the critics be damned.

Today, we don't typically have a psychological safety hatch of this kind to hand; there is no dominant idea that will tell us we are good and fine and right even though we might be degraded in the eyes of the wider world. Is it still possible to find inner security? Is there a psychological place of greater safety?

One beautiful clue lies in the word choice: 'greater' just means more than currently. It doesn't mean perfect, just a bit better.

One big move is the rational comprehension of others. Their hostility to us need not be based on powerful insight into our hopelessness; instead, they are taking out their own displaced failings on us.

Another route to greater safety is the knowledge that we all fail. We don't exit the human community by messing up; we join it.

Then there is the cosmic, and deeply true, idea that deep down none of this matters. We're a collection of neurotic ants crawling on the surface of a mid-sized planet on the fringes of an unremarkable galaxy.

Therefore, every time we dust the shelf or glance at the title, we are drawn back to the place we belong: the deeper, more creative recesses of our own minds.

Lossapardo, illustration for 'Notes
on Grief' by Chimamanda Ngozi Adichie,
published in *The New Yorker*, 2020

*When we read of the experience and
sorrow of another we are, ideally,
learning to think more accurately and
more generously about love and loss
in our own lives.*

Chimamanda Ngozi Adichie, *Notes on Grief*, 2021

There are books that are powerful not so much because of the particular story they tell but because they invite us to tell our own version. If we read the elegant and profound meditations and memories of Chimamanda Ngozi Adichie's *Notes of Grief*, it is perhaps because we want to make our own, less public, notes – and we turn to her for inspiration. There's one very particular theme she describes, as she addresses the death of her father, that may not only touch us deeply but get us to reflect on the wider world as well.

Adichie grew up in a well-to-do, sophisticated, fun-loving and intellectual family in Nigeria. She was educated at the best schools. She was stylish and popular; she won a place to study medicine. Then she decided to move to New York to join her older sister. She continued her academic career in the USA with distinction and flourished as a novelist and public intellectual. By the time she was 40, Adichie had received more than a dozen honorary degrees from some of the world's most prestigious universities. But she shared the same overwhelming sense of loss with every child of a beloved dead parent.

Grief has this odd aspect: it does not answer to what we are supposed to think. Adichie's father, a professor of statistics, was not particularly what current intellectual glamour would fantasise. He was strongly attached to his family's aristocratic traditions; he was a philosophical sceptic who doubted the real-world validity of idealistic solutions to any social problem. He wouldn't be receiving honorary degrees from progressive universities, and yet, she would have given anything to see him smile again or listen to his thoughts or have him put an arm around her shoulder.

We live in a world of supposed ideological divides in which it is almost a duty to think badly of those on the other side. The immensity of grief argues, via our deepest emotions, for a different view. We do not choose who we grieve for, but when grief strikes our life, we are dislodged from our simpler certainties. We realise we could desperately miss someone from across an ideological gulf and that, therefore, the gulf cannot be as important as we had imagined. We cannot any longer feel they are simply the enemy, for they could die.

Grief is love plus loss, and we might not have known the extent of our love until the loss taught us to feel it. Love is terrible at ideology, for love cannot judge another by their convictions – it attaches to something so much more fundamental about who they are. The aesthete loves their mother who doesn't give two hoots about the Renaissance; the intellectual loves their sport-mad sister.

It is one of the strangest truths of the human condition: grief can leave us genuinely wiser and kinder; in its face hate retreats.

VII.
Nature and
Science

IOAN. PICVS. MIRANDVLA·

Antonio Maria Crespi (known as Bustino),
*Portrait of Giovanni Pico della
Mirandola*, 1613–1621

*If we could feel properly proud of human
nature, we might start to behave with
greater responsibility towards the rest
of nature.*

Pico della Mirandola,
Oration on the Dignity of Man, 1486

It is almost an article of modern faith that we should feel collectively ashamed of ourselves. Stated extremely, we are a kind of planetary disease; to see ourselves as the highest point of creation, as the proper sovereigns of the earth and the rightful stewards of all its resources, is heresy. We're just an invasive species of great ape and 'Mother Nature' is now, rightly, fighting back. The logic of the argument is that we might start to behave more responsibly if only we could convince ourselves how worthless and unimportant we really are.

In the 15th century, the Italian philosopher Pico della Mirandola took the opposite view. He thought that if we fully recognised the dignity and wonder of being human, we might behave more nobly.

Psychologically, this is a dispute between two ideas about how to change people's behaviour: do we humiliate people into change or is a strategy of praise more effective? Do people change because we tell them how awful they currently are or because we invite them to live up to a higher vision of who they might be?

Born in 1463, Pico inherited the title of Lord of Mirandola. His inherited estate was halfway between Florence and Venice. He was rich, impossibly attractive and erotically adventurous. He could declaim all 10,000 lines of Dante's *Divine Comedy* backwards. Intellectually, he embraced fields that were seen as opposed. He loved the careful logic of medieval philosophy and the free-flowing elegance of the newly emerging literary style called humanism; he liked avant-garde ideas and traditional Jewish biblical studies; he was fascinated by the Quran and by the vulgar folk songs and stories of the day.

Oration on the Dignity of Man, written when Pico was in his early 20s, places human beings at the intersection of 'the beasts' – that is, all other living things – and 'the divine'. We are part god and part animal. Our minds are infinitely more subtle than that of any other creature. Our thoughts can range from the beginning of time to the end of all things; we can interrogate our own nature, question our own motives, wonder about meaning; we can reason and argue and change our minds; we are conscious of our own freedom to choose.

Today we may like to talk of the intelligence of whales and even of the wisdom of a forest, but this is an act of extreme generosity. Such cognitive powers are (as Pico would put it) narrow and inflexible; they cannot be self-directed and turned to new problems.

His point isn't to let us off the hook. It is because we're a great kind of being that we have great responsibility. It is because we alone have the capacity to imagine and discuss the future that we alone have a duty to do something about it. It is because we are glorious that we should also be good.

Books on Charles Darwin's desk,
Down House, Downe, Kent

*Our expectations of others, and of
ourselves, are too high, because we
forget where we've all come from.*

Charles Darwin,
The Descent of Man, 1871

It is understandable that we are often maddened by what might be called 'normal' humanity: the way in which emotion so regularly triumphs over careful reasoning; the power of group loyalty, even when the group doesn't seem to deserve much devotion; the vast mechanisms of status-seeking that drive so much excess consumption; widespread selfishness and indifference to the greater needs of more distant others. We can find ourselves, in the privacy of our own heads or in the occasional late-night outburst, railing against the fools and idiots who occupy so many of the prominent places of power, wealth and influence.

In such moods, Darwin has much to say to us. He was born in England in 1809 into a well-to-do and intellectually distinguished family. He was much influenced by visiting, in his 20s, the Galapagos Islands, where he could see at first hand species remarkably different from those that existed elsewhere. In later life he was a quiet, rather withdrawn man (he became the world's leading expert on barnacles). He achieved worldwide fame for his great work *On the Origin of Species by Means of Natural Selection*, but he felt that people had not quite understood the implications of his ideas. In 1871, when he was in his 60s, he brought out *The Descent of Man*.

Darwin liked to say that he had thought of calling his book *The Ascent of Man* but that that would suggest some idea of progress. Rather, he wanted to show that despite the obvious technical advances of past centuries, modern people were still at the same moral level as, or perhaps slightly worse than their remote ancestors.

His point is that the basic psychological characteristics of human beings evolved to aid survival in the remote past. At the simplest level, we are (generally) attracted to sweet things because in the very extended period of early human development that meant eating wild berries that are good for our health. It has only been in very recent times that this inbuilt desire has turned against us and given us a craving for sugar, which by Darwin's time had become a major industrial commodity.

We also evolved to be highly conscious of our position within our own immediate group, since so much of our survival in the past depended on that, so today being 'liked' feels as if it is a life-or-death issue because in the past it indicated whether you would be served when the spoils of the hunt were being distributed.

Practically everything then depended on having a mate and reproducing. So our minds are massively preoccupied by these questions, even though today they are not central to our individual survival or even our happiness. Obviously, emotive behaviour is much earlier and much more deeply rooted than elaborate reasoning, which is a very recent and still terribly fragile development in human culture.

We can put on clothes and drive in cars, but we still carry our primate heritage, and that, though disappointing, is not our fault. Darwin teaches us to feel compassion for the very large primitive part of who we all are.

Ruth Benedict, 1937

Every society, seen from the outside,
can seem strange. Because ours becomes
familiar, we find it hard to see just how
weird our customs and assumptions are.

Ruth Benedict,
The Chrysanthemum and the Sword, 1946

The world we are born into seems completely natural: it is simply how things are and have to be. But it can be a huge help to recognise just how historically odd, and arbitrary, the accepted habits of our own society are. It's not that we think things here will change radically any time soon; it's rather that we can come to see ourselves as potentially universal creatures who happen to have been consigned to a particular, and inevitably limited, culture. We could have been anything – and yet we're expected to think and feel like *this*.

For readers today, the delight of Ruth Benedict is that she takes us into what (in her view) it meant to be Japanese in the 1930s and 40s. As an outsider, she tries to specify the patterns of thought and feeling; what seemed natural at that time and in that place. She isn't so much shedding light on one moment of human civilisation as conveying something about *all* complex human societies.

Born in 1887 and educated in New York, Benedict wrote her PhD thesis at Columbia University and was one of the early proponents of anthropology as a way of studying modern societies. In 1944 the US government commissioned her to write a report on 'the mentality of Japan'.

Benedict loves small details. What happens if someone's hat blows off in the wind and lands at the feet of a stranger? In the USA, ideally, the stranger picks it up, brushes off the dust and returns it to its owner – a tiny act of courtesy. But as Benedict saw it in Japan this would be a much more fraught occasion. The hat-returner is doing a service and is therefore owed a heavy burden of gratitude – which could, in principle, last forever. To pick up the hat and give it back is to make a demand on the recipient. The polite thing, therefore, might be to leave the hat where it is and ignore what has happened.

Benedict was equally fascinated by the ending of Japanese films, which often avoided any kind of moral resolution; by how children see themselves as 'indebted' to their parents and by the intensity of the Japanese vision of respect as owed to *whoever* happened to be in charge.

The practicalities of her report were historically significant, guiding and encouraging much of the work of reconstruction that occurred in Japan after 1946. But for us the meaning is much more intimate. By seeing *one* society analysed we get a sense of how *any* society could be. There is no particular way a human being has to think or feel, no set standard of values or emotions; we're all living in artificial cultures. It's a shocking insight: our inner lives are more plastic, more absorbent of ambient influence, than we can reasonably imagine. We are born open to anything.

We needn't hate what we are; Benedict just wants us to be more alive to how radically 'other' we might have been.

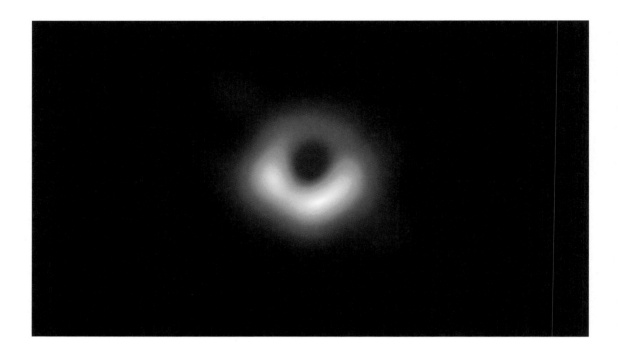

The first image of a black hole at the
centre of the galaxy M87, taken by the
Event Horizon Telescope, published
10 April 2019

There are joys to being a beginner.

Carlo Rovelli,
Seven Brief Lessons on Physics, 2014

We are conditioned to aspire to expertise and to be ashamed of our ignorance. But in the hands of the right teacher there are few things more exciting than starting almost from scratch. Every lesson is a huge revelation; each page opens our eyes. However late it is in our lives, it is not too late.

Physics is one of the hidden drivers of the world, but its achievements are complex and grand; unless we have a strong background, it seems almost humiliating to even try to engage.

Rovelli's little essays are written for absolute beginners. A distinguished and very charming Italian theoretical physicist, born in Verona in 1956, Rovelli is delighted if we know nothing of the second law of thermodynamics, because it gives him the chance to let us in on an amazing piece of cosmic gossip. His aim isn't to teach us all of what he knows, or even a small fraction of that; his aim is nobler and more thrilling: he wants us to share with him a feeling of delight at the beauty of the project of describing the ultimate, physical nature of reality. He gives us the dignity of being fellow travellers, joining him in his search, his doubts and hopes and his moments of revelation.

He gently but decisively introduces us to ideas that can clear up lingering confusions. At one point, he tries to define the remote origins of the scientific project. A lot of people, he says, imagine that science is about making up stories to make sense of our world, rather like the tales our ancestors recounted around the fire in the evenings for hundreds of thousands of years: of how the stars are the souls of our ancestors or how the divine spirit fashioned woman out of man's rib. No, he says:

Science is the continuation of something else: of the gaze of these same people – early in the morning – searching in the dust of the savannah for the hoof marks of an antelope; examining the details of what can actually be seen in order to deduce the existence of things that can't be seen directly: always aware they could be wrong and therefore ready at any moment to change their ideas if a new sign should turn up; but also knowing that if they're careful they'll be able to find what they're looking for – they'll eat that night.

There's no blame if we happened to suppose that science was like the campfire stories; just a gentle offer of a vivid and more accurate alternative.

Our world needs a million Rovellis, to teach us to dance, to sing, to cook, to do our accounts, to chat with our adolescent children, to manage our relationships with our phones – and with our partners. Our current ignorance and incapacity is no shame: it is the ideal starting point. Tragically there is as yet no major institution devoted to teaching people to do what he does: to convert intimidation into happy discovery.

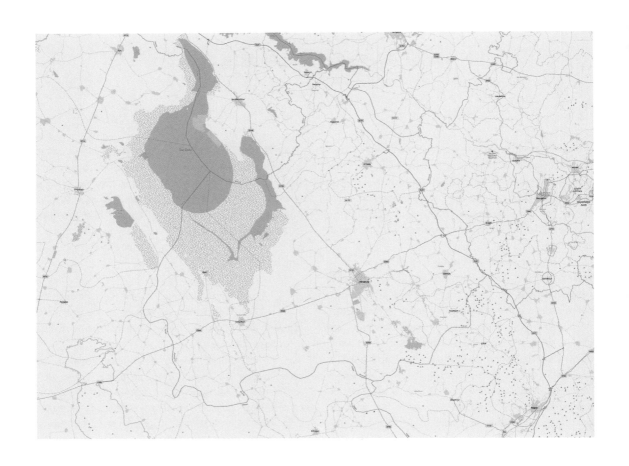

Aksaray, province of Turkiye, street map

*It's a huge relief to grasp how little we
know of our world.*

An Atlas of the World

The larger the pages and the more detail, the better. The point isn't to plan a route or remember somewhere we've been; what we're looking for is places that are unfamiliar.

This particular map, for instance, might be focused on the road network and population centres of Aksaray, one of the eighty-one administrative provinces of Turkiye; the main city, also called Aksaray, is located near Tuz Gölü, a large saline lake, which tends to dry up during the summer and provides over half of Turkiye's domestic salt. The Aksaray region is cold in the winter and hot in the summer, and annual rainfall is low; around seventy per cent of the region's population (which is growing steadily and will soon hit 450,000) are involved in agriculture. It takes about eight hours to drive northeast to Istanbul and about ten hours, mainly heading south, to reach the Palestinian city of Beirut.

We don't easily realise it, but our picture of the world suffers from multiple distortions. The places we know and the ones we tend to hear about represent only a select sliver of the inhabited globe. Although we may be familiar with a city name, in few cases have we any sense of the actual districts in which most people live.

Our mental image of 'London', for instance, is unlikely to include Cheshunt, a quiet, modest area on the far northern fringe of the city and fairly representative of the sort of place where most 'Londoners' actually live. While we may have an image of 'New York' imprinted on our minds by films and TV series, it probably doesn't include the leafy, low-density area of Waterbury, or the Naugatuck River on which it is situated.

An atlas invites us to notice the places that normally escape our attention: for instance, the small city of Salto in northwestern Uruguay or Kōchi Prefecture on the island of Shikoku, Japan. The atlas is our therapeutic mentor, gently reminding us that most places are not, and cannot possibly be, famous or known to us. Our picture of the lives of others, of the reality of their day-to-day lives, of their opinions, concerns, preoccupations and ambitions must be equally sketchy.

As we skim our atlas, it isn't sending us the stern (and actually insane) message that we have to be deeply informed about the entire world. Rather it's saying that we have to remember that we're not and can't be. We have, essentially, no idea what most people in the world are like, how they think and feel and what their views about anything might be, let alone what they might be like as individuals. (And, of course, we are 'they' to 'them'.)

The help is in letting us know that we don't know: our fears and hopeful expectations are equally likely to be misplaced. The atlas enfolds us in the relief of humility.

VIII.
The Arts and
Architecture

The *Cha-no-yu*, or Tea Ceremony, one
of the Esoteric Arts of Japan, from
*Tetsudōin, Sights and Scenes in Fair
Japan*, c. 1910–1919

'The spirit of tea' is the cure
for banality.

Kakuzo Okakura, *The Book of Tea*, 1906

The Japanese tea ceremony sounds wonderful but utterly removed from normal daily life. It is exotic, perfect and noble, while we are condemned to trudge from one lowly, dreary task to another.

This is the opposite of the therapeutic lesson Kakuzo Okakura longs to impart: as he sees it, anything can be 'tea'.

He was born in Yokohama in 1863, less than a decade after the Japanese elite elected to reconnect with the West after centuries of seclusion. He was an accomplished student at the newly established Tokyo University and was quickly appointed a curator at the, also recently founded, Imperial Museum of the Arts.

In 1906, when he was in his early 40s, Kakuzo Okakura moved to the USA to take up a post at the Boston Museum of Fine Art. He loved socialising but was saddened by how his otherwise cultivated friends misunderstood Japanese art and philosophy, which he saw as intimately linked. He quickly wrote (in English) and published (in 1906) this charming little book to explain what he saw as a central concern of Japanese culture.

The 'secret' and 'fascination' (as he often heard it called) of the tea ceremony turns out to have little or nothing to do with tea itself: it's not a way of revering a special beverage. It's almost irrelevant that the 'ceremony' involves a hot drink. What matters is the rituals that happened to grow up around this. Any simple thing can become the focus for endless meaning. One waits patiently as the water boils, notices the wisps of steam and appreciates the implements (which should be very simple) and the sounds. The 'ceremony' is calm and ordered, people are served according to a special order. The room is small, almost humble, but tranquil and spotlessly clean. It's the attitude that he wants to convey: the sensitivity to detail, the liking for solid, well-made things, the avoidance of complexity or haste, the devotion to the moment.

The same attitude can be cultivated in other areas: flowers are arranged in the same spirit, noticing each stem, caring about the spaces between them, taking time to appreciate them, concentrating solely on their silent loveliness. But, again, this is not because flowers are 'special'. What's special is the way something is done: thoughtfully, beautifully, simply and with a sense of eternity. The point is to concentrate on now, rather than to be preoccupied with what may or may not happen in the future.

More or less anything can be done in this spirit. You could take a 'tea' approach to driving, or to cooking, or to brushing your teeth: pushing the ideal amount of paste out of the tube; learning to appreciate, perhaps, a slightly granular texture or silky consistency; holding the brush neither too stiffly nor too loosely; being conscious of the intricate sensations, aware that this moment is now and that now is part of forever. It's not an activity in itself that is banal or spiritual, it's only our approach, our way of doing it, that makes it so.

Trevi Fountain, Rome

*We can trust our own experience more
around great works of art.*

Heinrich Wölfflin,
Principles of Art History, 1915

When we know we are looking at a famous creative masterpiece we tend to get nervously dutiful and artificially intellectual: we register, from a guidebook or our phone, the date the work was created; we feel we should try to remember the name of the artist or designer and we somehow try to follow a few remarks about stylistic predecessors, patrons and subsequent influences. Essentially, we've absorbed a seemingly authoritative message: until we learn enough facts (which we probably never will), we had better be cagey and guarded, and deferential to experts, in our responses. We're trying to do the right thing, but the end result is that we feel emotionally deadened and disconnected around works that are supposed to be thrilling.

In such difficult moments, our therapeutic friend is Heinrich Wölfflin. He was born in Winterthur in Switzerland in 1864, and went on to have a distinguished academic career as an art historian in Munich and later in Zurich. Despite being immensely learned, Wölfflin came to the conclusion that the best, and most important, strategy for engaging with art and architecture is to ignore names and dates and instead simply to look more closely and carefully at what we see directly in front of us. *Kunstgeschichtliche Grundbegriffe (Principles of Art History)* first published in Germany in 1915, is his account of what we should ideally be doing with our eyes – and our emotions – when we meet a new painting or building.

He wants us to look at the work and ask ourselves some questions about what the creator seemed to like or enjoy: what excited them? What gave them pleasure?

Are they attracted to airy and light shapes, or do they prefer a more solid and massy effect? Do they like building up to a crescendo in the middle, or do they prefer spreading their attention out smoothly and equally across all the parts of what they made, so it's more like a simple melody? Are they attracted to serenity, or do they like being more passionate and demonstrative? Are they excited by a sense of power and force, or are they more charmed by delicacy and gentleness?

In effect he's asking us to look for the visual personality of the object: if the work was a person, what sort of person might they be?

When we encounter a work of art, we are, in effect, being made an offer of friendship. As in the rest of life, we don't have to be friends with everyone; it will be personality, rather than names and dates, that forms the foundation of intimacy. We're not always looking for an image of ourselves: we may be prone to agitation and therefore appreciate the company of a more mellow companion; we may be short on confidence but feel bolstered in the company of a more self-assured ally; we're in search of a soulmate who happens to be made of coloured canvas or of stone.

Le Corbusier, *Recherches sur les unités d'habitation*, façade sketch showing the brise-soleils, 1944. Le Corbusier's theories of the housing unit led to his tower blocks, the Unités d'habitation

We often don't realise the degree to which our thinking and our imagination are constrained by habit.

Le Corbusier,
The Radiant City, 1935

We often stick with the preconceptions that have, by chance, been instilled in us by our individual and collective past; we are loyal to what happens to be familiar. We very rarely go back, as it were, to the drawing board and think things out afresh for ourselves.

Born in 1887, Charles-Édouard Jeanneret is our guide to the reverse attitude: he was desperate to rethink, from the ground up, everything that had once been held dear.

He grew up in Switzerland, where his father was a moderately successful watchmaker. In his 20s he travelled around Europe, taking up training positions in architectural firms in Budapest, Vienna and Florence, then settled permanently in Paris when he was 30. It was around this time that he adopted a new name, Le Corbusier, in line with his idea that the future should not be determined by the past.

Initially he designed villas for the well-to-do. He loved simple, clean spaces, free of ornament and clutter; he was inspired by the functional elegance of sports cars, ocean liners, factories and the first aeroplanes – things that seemed gloriously modern and weren't beholden to tradition.

But following World War I, he became concerned with mass housing. Outside their small affluent areas, old cities weren't much better than the trenches: they were squalid, overcrowded, unsanitary, with never a tree or a wide-open green space to be seen. Le Corbusier began to have revolutionary ideas. It was no good tinkering with the details; cities would have to be reinvented.

In 1925 he went public with a grand, and instantly rejected, proposal to pull down most of Paris and replace it with tower blocks set in landscaped gardens. Later, in 1935, he explained the thinking behind the project in a book: *La Ville Radieuse* (*The Radiant City*). He imagined office workers commuting home (reading, perhaps, a little poetry on the train) and having a cocktail on the terrace of their small but beautifully organised flat, before heading to a Stravinsky concert in the cultural quarter. Life would be rational, refined, cultivated and efficient for everyone. We could eradicate the past and start again and get it right this time.

When eventually, after a further catastrophic war, his ideas were widely taken up, and widely copied, the reality didn't align with his vision. His ideal of collective housing was for every kind of person; the postwar blocks accommodated only the poor and were ill-served by transport; few cocktail parties were held on the raw concrete terraces he had so carefully argued for. Many buildings inspired by his visions have been detonated.

We are not trying to be exactly like him. But Le Corbusier has something helpful to say to us all the same. We can't personally reinvent the world, but we may need to reinvent our marriage or our relationship to our son or our attitude to work. We want these to be more radiant, to shine more. It's the architecture of our lives, rather than our cities, that we may be inspired to redesign.

Brenda Prince, *Marion Milner*, 1997

*How can we be not much good at something
and yet get great satisfaction from
doing it? How do we turn a fear into an
enthusiasm?*

Marion Milner,
On Not Being Able to Paint, 1950

In a world where being good at things is always alluring, and where competitive success can feel central to our identity and status, it's strangely exciting and helpful to encounter someone who is eager to explore, in public, something at which they are distinctly amateurish.

Born in 1900, Marion Milner was strongly competitive by nature. Brought up in the exact middle of the middle class, she was exceptionally good and hard-working at school; at university she was a model student. But in the background there was the compelling figure of her slightly older brother. He was unconventional, he didn't know what he wanted to do, so he tried out various low-grade jobs before turning to physics, which he was spectacularly good at, rapidly gaining a professorship at Cambridge and, eventually, a Nobel Prize.

For a person trying to be very good, this is a strange and difficult example to have at such close quarters. The example is tantalising: let yourself wander, try out weird things. But how can we risk taking that path, unless we turn out in the end (like her brother) to be exceptionally brilliant? It's a touching question for certain of us: how can we like doing things we're never going to get the world's approval for? Can we learn to love things just because we happen to like them, irrespective of what anyone else thinks?

For Milner, the problem arose around drawing. She wanted to draw but hated the drawings she actually did. She'd draw a tree and feel it was the worst drawing anyone had ever done. She couldn't bear to look at her own work and summed up her style as 'boring'.

But she discovered a solution: she'd stop trying to draw or paint good pictures and simply let her unconscious motives have free rein. On one crucial occasion she set herself up to paint a beautiful meadow and started adding flames to the trees. She wasn't drawing what she actually saw but expressing something hidden inside her. Or she'd try to paint a picture of a bird but end up doing an imaginary portrait of a witch. In 1950 she turned her lonely self-criticism, and eventual acceptance, into a book.

The point wasn't to become a great or successful artist: no one was remotely interested in buying her work. Rather, she started to really enjoy doing it. She wasn't seeking approval from anyone and she wasn't trying to impress anyone. The hard thing had been to enthuse herself and now she'd worked out how to do that. She painted from her darker imagination: the part of her that had hitherto found so little opportunity for expression in her careful and correct life.

Our own version may be to explore our inability to dance, or sing, or contact a friend to ask them round, or to face our tax returns or weed the garden. We don't need to get good; we just need to be less appalled by our limited capacities. If we like, we could even write our new skill on our tombstone.

Dick Bruna, *Miffy at the Zoo*, cover
of edition published in 1955

We already understand all about art.

Dick Bruna,
Miffy at the Zoo, 1955

One of the peculiar tragedies of the modern world is the promotion of the idea that 'art' is too rarefied and complicated for most people, us included, to really enjoy. Art, it seems, has become ever more 'sophisticated' and distant from ordinary experience. We feel unqualified, and too scared, to offer an opinion. Yet the truth is we've known all about art since our childhoods and, at its best, it has the power to touch us all.

In 1955, a Dutch illustrator, Dick Bruna, whose family had long been involved in publishing, brought out a book he'd written himself that, he feared, no one would like. It was intended for the youngest readers and the story, about a little rabbit going on a nice, ordinary visit to the zoo, wasn't the problem. What he was worried about was the illustrations.

Bruna was a great fan of the stark simplicity of artistic modernism and was inspired particularly by Mondrian and Matisse and their devotion to precise geometry, blocks of plain colour and simple outlines. At the time this was seen as a style that only radical members of the avant-garde could appreciate. It was seen as too revolutionary, controversial and demanding for the average member of the public, and now Bruna, perhaps insanely, was trying to use it in a book aimed at young children.

But the book – and the many others Bruna wrote and illustrated in the same way – became immensely popular. It turned out that preschoolers around the world, who knew nothing about art theory or cutting-edge art history, were charmed by the images.

When we return to Miffy we're not looking for high literary drama; we're reconnecting with the origins of our interest in art and beauty. We were little and yet we loved such images. We were already connoisseurs and experts. We were alive to the most central thing any artwork ever does: touch our hearts by visual means. Such natural confidence is innate and yet gets squashed by the social prestige and aura of intellectual complexity by which art comes to be surrounded.

It could be wished that every great gallery in the world would have a Miffy illustration in the entry lobby. Not because it's the deepest or most perfect thing ever created, but because it sets the right benchmark: we already have an inbuilt feel for art. This is our home territory; we've been natives since before we can remember. It says, in effect: bring your Miffy-inspired sensitivity here and see if anything appeals.

It's a strangely moving proposal: the great high points of cultural achievement may be so great not because they are accessible only to the elevated and especially instructed few but because they strike a chord with universal human nature. Their delights are, therefore, open to us all, 4-year-olds included.

Kenneth Clark, *Civilisation*, cover
of edition published in 1969

*We are allowed to love beauty,
splendour and artistic perfection.*

Kenneth Clark, *Civilisation*, 1969

It is fairly standard now to feel we should be wary of the word 'civilisation'. We've come to suppose that it's shameful to assert the greatness of certain things. And while this originates in kindness, it can also leave us slightly depressed. The worry is that to revel in the grandeur and visual charm of certain human achievements in the arts and architecture is to forget the darker, grimmer aspects of history and of human societies.

In these times of doubt, Kenneth Clark is our intimate, supportive friend. In 1969, when he was in his mid-60s, he presented a BBC television series that set out to display the finest accomplishments of Western art. The following year, the transcripts were published as this book.

Clark's view is almost directly the opposite of modern worries, but for the least expected reason. He adored the pinnacles of art not because he was ignorant of human failings but because he was so aware of them. He, like most of his audience, had lived through both World War I and II. Human monstrosity was a truth so obvious as to hardly need stating. And he knew very painfully how appalling and cruel the rich could be: his own father – a notorious drunk and domestic tyrant – was a perfect example.

Clark was born in 1903, the only child of a wealthy family, the family firm being at the time the world's second largest supplier of zips. He rose rapidly in the art world, becoming the director of the National Gallery in London when he was only 30, though he likened the day-to-day work to that of running a large department store. Then, in 1966 – when The Rolling Stones and The Beatles were approaching almost universal fame and Clark was nearing 65 – a youthful controller of programmes at the BBC, a certain David Attenborough (who went on to become one of the most beloved presenters in history), asked him to make an expansive series about the high points of Western culture. It turned out to be immensely popular around the world, especially in the USA.

What Clark means, ultimately, by 'civilisation' is an energetic, confident devotion to the gentlest, most intelligent and most exciting parts of our own nature. The objects that feed and encourage this devotion speak sensuously and powerfully to us, irrespective of where and when they originated. We spread ourselves out over time and space and find that objects that we thought had only a scholarly interest turn out to be addressing our own spiritual and imaginative needs. We can feel close, where we once felt distant. The great things are ours and belong equally to everyone.

Clark could see that the dismantling of high culture would not benefit 'the masses'. It would simply remove one more fetter from capitalism and empower the rich to be unashamedly vulgar. Beauty doesn't belittle others; the cruelty is to say that what is gracious or tender or noble is irrelevant to any but a few.

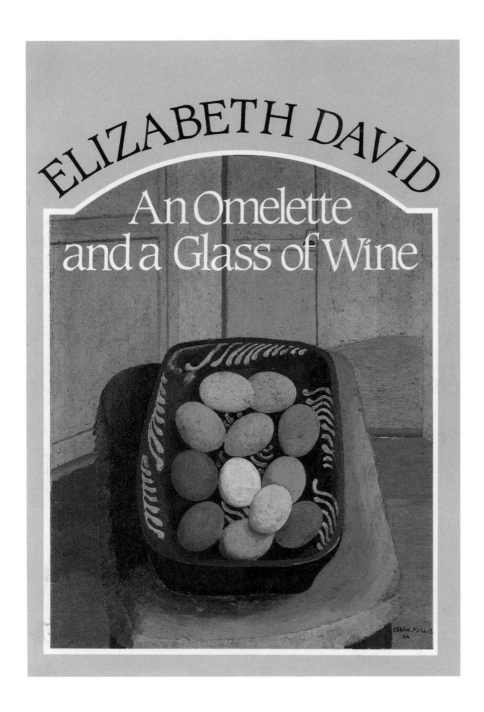

Elizabeth David, *An Omelette and a
Glass of Wine*, cover of edition published
in 1985

*We can stop endorsing the preferences
of others and start asserting our own
independent and authentic tastes.*

Elizabeth David,
An Omelette and a Glass of Wine, 1984

One of the oddities of the human condition is the degree to which we sacrifice our own enjoyment to what we think others *think* is enjoyable. There is perhaps no more precise temple to our folly than the chic restaurant that serves complex, elaborate dishes. We feel we ought to be delighted, though often we're not – and we feel compelled to tell others how marvellous it all was. We say we adore the sophisticated and the rare because we lack confidence in our own direct experience, which tells us that what we really like is often simple and straightforward.

A great ally and supporter of our beleaguered convictions was Elizabeth David. Born Elizabeth Gwynne in 1913, she came from an aristocratic background but elected to live a wildly adventurous and often chaotic life. She studied in Paris, lived on a Greek island and, in her late 20s, during World War II, was briefly 'married' to a certain very dashing Mr David – who turned out to be married already. Subsequently she had many intense, usually disastrous, love affairs. She was immensely outspoken and often deeply frustrated. She never made much money and at one point had to live in a single room. A grander friend commented that she was cooking in her bedroom. 'No,' she replied, 'I'm sleeping in the kitchen.' She died, in her late 70s, in 1992.

During the 1950s Elizabeth David wrote a popular food and cooking column for a major UK newspaper. The origin of the particular essay we're focusing on was a teasing question she always wanted to ask her readers: *what was your best meal ever?* She could guess what the answers would be: some sumptuous occasion at one of the world's most expensive establishments, or an ultra-exotic dish prepared uniquely in the foothills of the Himalayas.

Her own choice could hardly be more different. It was the most common of dishes, a humble omelette. And she'd had it in a modest, out-of-the-way restaurant no one had ever heard of. She even gave the recipe: 'get some good eggs, and some good butter, make an omelette in a good pan, eat it'.

The grand philosophical point she had in view was simply that it takes a weird degree of confidence to assert that you like something that has no external support. Prior to her, no one had given the place she ate magnificent reviews, no one had been saying that this omelette was the crown of cuisine or asserting that a one-line recipe was sufficient for gastronomic excellence. Her therapeutic glory was to rely on her own pleasure.

For her it was a maddening, perverse consequence of her article that, for a while, omelettes became chic and that the restaurant became famous. That wasn't her point. We were not supposed to be imitating her preferences but to be having more confidence in our own. Her genuine pleasure seemed weird. Ours might be too – and that's precisely what she wanted to encourage.

IX.
Coffee Table
Books

Engraving by Bernard Picart, *Villa Rotunda,* in Andrea Palladio, *The Architecture of A. Palladio in Four Books containing a Short Treatise on the Five Orders*, edition published in 1715

We've been duped into valuing innovation over beauty.

Andrea Palladio,
The Four Books of Architecture, 1570

Copying is seen as shameful in modern culture. To simply reproduce an earlier model is, we're told, the opposite of creativity. The artist or designer is supposed to be radically innovative and to shock us with their new ideas. It sounds marvellous, until we recall that almost all the great art of the world has been made by people who felt the opposite: they were avowed traditionalists. We don't have to make an absolute commitment to one side or the other, but it might be helpful to remind ourselves, occasionally, of the case for sticking with a good idea, even if it is an old one.

A figure we can turn to is an Italian architect working, and writing, in the 1500s: Andrea di Pietro della Gondola (Palladio was a classical nickname he adopted later in life). He was born in Padua, not far from Venice, in 1508. He came from a modest background and in his teens became an apprentice stonemason. It wasn't until he was in his 30s, and happened to be doing some work for a cultivated and imaginative patron who took him under his wing, that he started on the path to being an architect. Following several instructive trips to Rome to view the remains of the great classical buildings, Palladio received a handful of prestigious commissions for churches and villas. The results are among the most loved and influential buildings in the history of architecture.

His *Four Books* is the record of all his projects. The written text is banal but is accompanied by a large number of detailed technical drawings – and this is where its glory lies. The drawings are instructions: they show precisely how to build as he did. He took himself to be copying from classical Roman buildings and, over the next three centuries, many later architects were content to copy his ideas. For instance, Thomas Jefferson, third president of the USA, owned a copy of *Four Books* and lifted his design for the University of Virginia, one of the loveliest university campuses in the world, straight from Palladio. The architects of Bath, Edinburgh and St Petersburg – three of the visually most charming cities on the planet – were also guided by his ideas.

There always has been – and should be – a tussle between innovators and traditionalists. When we're ruled by technology it feels obvious that innovation must always be the road to genuine improvement. Yet, increasingly, we're realising that this is not the case: new doesn't automatically mean better or wiser. Palladio sits on our coffee table as a reminder that keeping on doing the same thing can be wonderful. He's a counterweight to a bias of modernity: in a world addicted to innovation, we need to have representatives of the opposite case.

The Constitution of the United States of
America, 1787

Some problems are impossible to solve.

The Constitution of the United States of America, 1787

In the summer of 1787, a committee was established to create a constitution for the USA. In the Revolutionary War (1775–1783) Americans had liberated themselves from the UK, but what form would their new society take? It was the task of this committee to define the deepest, most permanent rules to govern the country.

The document, ultimately composed by James Madison, a successful farmer from Virginia, but developed in collaboration with such impressive figures as Thomas Jefferson, Benjamin Franklin and George Washington, was as considerate and thoughtful as any constitution could possibly be. They tried to learn as carefully as possible from historical experience; they sought to overcome the formidable problems they saw in other societies.

Of course, it's not a book to leaf through for pleasure, even if we omit the massive additions that were made in the form of Amendments over the next two centuries. Its therapeutic value to us isn't to do with everything it says, but with something it stands for. And that is the impossibility of solving all problems at the same time.

A particularly maddening feature turns up right at the start. In Article I it is stated that all States of the Union will have equal representation in the Senate, and therefore equal voices in all future legislation. This was deemed necessary because otherwise the individual states would have no great incentive to join or stay in the union. But from a democratic point of view this was an absurdity. It means today that California, with a population approaching 40 million, has the same Senatorial status as Wyoming, with a population just under 600,000: they each get two votes. And the system can't plausibly be changed because to amend it would require the agreement of senators from a large number of states that would, in effect, be annihilated by this revision.

Equally, the extremely intelligent idea of separating the branches of government was designed to prevent the over-concentration of power, which opens the way to tyranny. But in doing so they created the conditions in which there would often be too little concentrated power, meaning that a president elected by the whole nation would be unable to push through a programme for which there seemed to be clear public support. When a president we support is in the White House this seems terrible, but when the office-holder strikes us as a menace this safeguard feels welcome. The point is: what else could the original framers of the Constitution have done? They were trying to resolve two opposed worries, both of which are serious – and perhaps there is simply no way of finding an ideal answer to both at the same time.

This overall picture of irresolvable tensions may apply widely across existence. We think if we solve one problem, things will get better, but we may simply have aggravated a major difficulty elsewhere. The promotion creates greater stress; not getting the promotion induces a sense of failure. The divorce liberates us but leaves us lonelier than before.

René Magritte, *Les Vacances de Hegel*
(Hegel's Holidays), 1958

We will never understand it in detail;
we may struggle to comprehend what is
actually being said on any particular
page, and yet we can love a book and need
it in our lives.

G.W.F. Hegel,
The Phenomenology of Spirit, 1807

Georg Wilhelm Friedrich Hegel was the dominant figure in early 19th-century German philosophy. His work, unfortunately, is not merely difficult to read; it is absurdly, insanely hard to follow. To include a work by Hegel in our therapeutic library is not to make the claim that we will carefully go through it line by line. Yet its accepted presence, its inclusion, is a powerful reminder to ourselves: not everything that needs to be said can, by this person, be said elegantly and quickly.

Clarity and easy comprehension are profoundly important, yet there are also important things that are too hard to say straightforwardly. We know it in ourselves: under pressure and feeling anxious, we try to say what we mean but we know we're not getting through; we can't find the logical, simple, convincing words. But it would be wrong to conclude that we don't have anything *worth* saying just because we can't say it well.

We can sometimes extend this generosity to others: the friend who stumbles their way through an account of why a relationship failed; our adolescent child trying to say how they see their future. We can accept that, sometimes, the issue is so complex, and the obstacles to truth so great, that what someone says might be baffling and yet we know they are trying to tell us something important.

Touchingly, Hegel himself has an explanation as to why this is the case: *the owl of Minerva spreads its wings only at dusk.* What he means is that, often, we only understand things at the end. We have to live through much of existence in conflict and confusion; we might have to wait a long time for Minerva, the classical Roman symbol of clear understanding, to manifest itself.

To love understanding is not to pretend that everything is as clear as we would like; it's an aspiration that will often be thwarted. Hegel was remarkably intelligent and yet to him the human condition appeared so confused and obscure that in his attempt to do it justice his writing is confused and obscure. We might on occasions skim his work, glancing here and there at his bewildering prose: 'for a spiritual notion to have an effect on the body it must, qua cause, be itself corporeal' (to take a random example). We don't conclude he was an idiot, only that it can be exceptionally difficult for clever people to tell us what they mean, and for us to tell them what we mean.

The Phenomenology of Spirit is in our library as a symbol. It stands for our willingness to bear with the struggle (which often fails) to put what we mean into words that are readily followed by others. We can be *trying* to say something that's important to us, even if we don't succeed. Our failure isn't the mark of our stupidity but of the inherent complexity of existence. And we know, as we glance at the book, that we are in the best of company.

Long Live the Thoughts of Chairman Mao,
propaganda poster from the Chinese
Cultural Revolution, September 1969

*If one could force practically everyone
to read a book, what would it be?*

Mao Tse-tung,
Quotations from Chairman Mao Tse-tung, 1964

Better known as *The Little Red Book* because of its distinctive cover, published initially in 1964, it has perhaps been reproduced more frequently than any other book of the 20th century, with claims that over 6 billion copies and translations have been printed.

Born in 1893, Mao, who was from a prosperous family and well educated, became a foundational member of the Communist Party and of its military wing, the Red Army, in his 30s, becoming the absolute ruler of China in 1949 after immense struggles. He remained in power until his death in 1976.

The Little Red Book was compiled and published as part of what was called the Cultural Revolution: the idea that to transform society, it is not enough that the economy is altered; everyone must share a certain set of convictions and attitudes.

The great meaning of this book isn't particularly to do with what it explicitly says. The contents – hundreds of brief extracts from the speeches and writings of Mao – are often just bald, dated ideological assertions:

- *The Chinese Communist Party is the core of leadership of the whole Chinese people. Without this core, the cause of socialism cannot be victorious.*

- *Without socialisation of agriculture, there can be no complete, consolidated socialism.*

Its significance is, rather, to do with its ambition. Everyone was required to read it; you could be prosecuted for not carrying a copy. To distribute it so widely, the Party set up thousands of printing factories and commandeered all the ink and paper.

We may have no interest in seeing the world transformed according to the specific ideas of Mao, but the idea that a book could (and perhaps might) be required reading for everyone is strangely enticing. Imagine similar priority being given to richer, more human works: a government that could deploy all its resources (and utilise the police) to ensure that everyone possesses a copy of, and has a good acquaintance with, Tolstoy or Proust or Virginia Woolf. Imagine a future in which a person might be arrested for not being able to quote Dante or Goethe or for venturing from home without a volume of Keats' selected poetry in their pocket …

We have become aware that horrible people might be ambitious when it comes to spreading their opinions and ideas; the thought that the genuinely wise and good things of the world could be the focus of an equally dramatic and well-organised resources drive feels almost impossible.

The promise of Mao's book isn't that we would adopt his particular tenets but that we could be as determined as he was to spread better ideas. When we imagine massive campaigns we tend to imagine the worst. But logically (and hopefully) it could be the finest things that were being shoved into everyone's pocket: grace and kindness, a willingness to engage with complexity, to imagine the other side of an argument, to wonder, seriously, if one might be wrong, to appreciate beauty, to grasp the hidden difficulties of other people's lives. These would no longer be tentative individual concerns, but the focus of the greatest state-sponsored ideas campaign of all time.

Sophie Bassouls, *James Baldwin in
Paris*, 1972

Sometimes we should definitely flee.

James Baldwin,
The Devil Finds Work, 1976

Running away from conflict and certain kinds of responsibility doesn't sound like a particularly adult or wise thing to do. Sometimes we know, secretly, we have to go, yet we feel it's shameful. We worry it means we're admitting defeat.

There's a kind of therapy that doesn't involve going in detail through the arguments pro or contra an exit. It consists simply of the example of someone obviously very admirable who fled. Our frank admiration of them helps strengthen our own resolve.

The long essay *The Devil Finds Work* contains a beautiful, painful account of James Baldwin's inner life growing up as a child in Harlem. It charts with horrifying precision his immense bewilderment as a 7-year-old that so many white adults, who might be very nice in lots of ways, could treat him badly because he was black: 'a child is far too self-centred to relate to any dilemma which does not, somehow, relate to him' – meaning: there are of course grim historical factors that promote cruelty but, at the intimacy level of a child, this makes no sense. It is as if one has been born into the wrong kind of world. And Baldwin already loved elegance and romantic intensity and adored Joan Collins. There's an almost unbearable tension between his delicacy of thought and perception and the brutality to which he was subjected.

But the ultimate power of the book may not reside in the fineness of its prose style but in a blunt fact: he wrote it in France. Practically penniless, he'd moved to Paris in 1948. He was in his mid-20s and there encountered a different, more hospitable world. His literary interests were normal, his homosexuality wasn't a problem. It wasn't that France was a multi-racial paradise, but that its cultural attitudes were more sophisticated.

Baldwin started his literary career and quickly found success. He was to stay in France for most of his adult life, moving in his 40s to a very charming house in Provence, where his friends often came to stay. It was there that he wrote this essay.

Flight isn't any kind of political policy; it's a private option that can't be a rule for everyone. But in our individual actions we are often right to prioritise our own survival and flourishing. There may very well be a better 'elsewhere'.

America taught Baldwin that the most significant thing about him was the colour of his skin – and, beyond that, that his sexuality defined him. What he seems to have encountered in Paris, and later the south of France, was that other aspects of who he was might be considered more important.

This is a historically and politically heightened version of what we may all be seeking: a true home. Too often we feel bound to stay in a relationship where our conviviality is a negative rather than a positive; in a job where our imagination is a drawback rather than an asset. We're trying to find the place where who we happen to be isn't an obstacle to our flourishing. Baldwin urges us to keep searching for our version of 'France'.

Alice in Genderland

"Poignant, honest, amazing...
Finally a pull-no-punches memoir
by a crossdresser in search
of himself and the truth."
— Gina Lance, Editor-In-Chief,
GIRL TALK magazine

Richard J. Novic, M.D.

Richard J. Novic, *Alice in Genderland*,
cover of edition published in 2005

*The thrill of who we might be, if we
weren't afraid.*

Richard J. Novic,
Alice in Genderland, 2004

Social inhibition and fear of what others might think are some of the most deep-rooted human emotions. We're social creatures and have evolved to be attuned to the reactions of those around us. It's an instinct that often serves us well, yet at times it threatens to ruin our lives. The crisis comes when something we fear will shock and disappoint others isn't wicked or cruel but simply a little odd.

When Richard Novic was growing up in the USA in the 1970s and 80s, he knew he wanted to wear girls' clothes. This was, so far as he could tell, an odd inclination. He didn't know that any other boys or men might have similar longings or, indeed, act them out. The agony of his early years revolved around the sense that 'unusual' is another way of saying 'bad'.

What made things especially difficult is that by ordinary standards he was what a boy was ideally supposed to be: sporty, ambitious and good at maths. He wasn't obviously an outsider, so the cost of revealing his seemingly strange inclinations was especially high. He did exceptionally well at school, he went to Harvard, he stayed on to qualify in medicine and then specialised in psychiatry. It was, outwardly, an ideal progression. For him, the withdrawal of social respect was especially terrifying for the simple fact that he had so much to lose.

We struggle with how to combine our extraordinary selves and our more conventional longings. Novic wanted some very standard things: to have an interesting, well-paid job, to be in a stable marriage with a woman he loved, to have a family – and to combine all that with the erotic and romantic adventure of being 'Alice'. *Alice in Genderland* is a description of a solution. Novic eventually found a female partner willing to start a family and to let him have one night a week as someone else.

The book is much bigger than its central theme. Although it describes powerfully what it's like to be a respectable man who loves makeup and heels, it more widely addresses the fear of rejection. Technically we live in a world that is very positive about people's choices. But in reality we inhabit microcommunities made up of our families, friends, neighbours, casual acquaintances, colleagues, employers and employees.

Novic's position isn't that we should overtly assert whatever we want, but that we should, like him, embrace tact, discretion, careful, quiet explanation and compromise. The majority have no duty to accommodate us, and we shouldn't hate them for not understanding. Our task isn't to force the world to convert but to search out the nonconflictual ways in which we can be ourselves without having to damage everything else we care about.

X.
Essays

1. Hofrath H. Meyer. 2. Frau v. Fritsch, geb. v. Wolfskul. 3. J. R. v. Goethe. 4. G. R. v. Einsiedel. 5. Herzogin Anna Amalia. 6. Frl. Elise Gore. 7. Charles Gore.
8. Frl. Emilie Gore. 9. Frl. v. Göchhausen. 10. Praes. v. Herder.

Georg Melchior Kraus, *Soirée at the residence of Duchess Anna Amalia of Saxe-Weimar*, c. 1795. From left to right: H. Meyer, Frau von Fritsch, Goethe, Einsiedel, Anna Amalia, Elise Gore, Charles Gore, Emilie Gore, Frl. v. Göchhausen and Herder

The charms of (cultivated) provincial life.

Germaine de Staël, *Weimar*, 1810

Sometimes we might be haunted by the idea that we're living in the wrong place. We may tell ourselves we're mired in a provincial nowhere and we dream of a new and better life in one of the world's great cities. This is not the kind of distress that invites universal sympathy. We're not starving or being hounded by the state police. Yet it is a real, if personal, issue.

A lovely companion in our life-is-elsewhere angst is the once towering, but now generally forgotten, Germaine de Staël, known to her family and friends as Minette.

She understood very well the allure of the great capitals. In the late 18th century she grew up – precariously – in the salons of Paris, then thought to be the very centre of the civilised world. Her mother was a socialite, her father the most important person in global finance. Her adolescence was passed chatting to representatives of the great world: ambassadors, prime ministers and the literary stars of the epoch.

Then history intervened: there was the French Revolution of 1789 and, a few years later, the rise to power of Napoleon Bonaparte. Both found fault with her: for the revolution she was too much of a moderate; for Napoleon, too much of an individualist. As a result, she spent many years in exile from Paris – far from the seeming centre of everything. She spent ages wishing she could return. Then, towards the end of the first decade of the 1800s, she had a revelation. Maybe she'd misunderstood. Maybe the great cities were overrated.

The focus of her new insight was the tiny provincial town of Weimar, located south of Berlin and east of Leipzig. It was almost inaccessible due to the poor condition of the roads; with a population of only 6,000, it was economically insignificant and politically backward; it was the back of beyond in the eyes of the sophisticated world and yet, after staying there for several weeks, she concluded that it was the most civilised place in Europe.

As she saw it, a few women in the town had generated a wonderful conversational atmosphere. People talked not to be admired (the vice of Paris), but to explain themselves. They weren't trying to dazzle; they were simply stating, in the most reasonable, calm and accurate terms, why they thought as they did.

It seems such a slight thing. She wasn't judging Weimar by GDP or armaments spending or the state constitution but simply asking: what is it like, here, when people talk to each other? This lovely talking culture was not some fantastic endowment from the gods; it was the creation of two women who had properly identified the kinds of conversations they wanted and encouraged a few others who, in turn, had spread the idea.

We may feel we long for another place when really we long for another way of talking to people.

Gottlieb Schick, *Apollo Among the Shepherds*, 1806-1808

What has happened to our childhood selves?

Heinrich Heine,
The Gods in Exile, 1854

We used to be so different; not just physically, of course, but psychologically. As children, perhaps, we loved spinning madly round the room to ABBA; now we can't even be dragged onto the dance floor. A game of hide-and-seek was thrilling, but it doesn't cross our minds to suggest playing it now with our friends. Once we spent ages drawing, but now we haven't done one for years. We loved playing football or scrambling up a tree or turning a cupboard into a cosy little house. It can sometimes feel as if these parts of us have simply vanished, to be replaced by the caution and sober demands of adult life.

Heine wants to tell us it's not so: these parts of us still exist and are longing to return to action, if only we'll let them.

Born in Düsseldorf in 1797, Heine grew up in a commercially minded family, started his career in his uncle's banking firm and then trained as a lawyer – but he was hopelessly out of place. He gave voice to his frustrations in satirical (and sometimes very rude) poems about conformism and the worship of authority. Eventually, as he was nearing 40, he fled to Paris, where his second cousin Karl Marx was already living. They were close for a while, but eventually Heinrich started to worry that grace, beauty, wit and the elegant daybeds on which he liked to recline would be banished under the dictatorship of the proletariat for which Karl was scheming.

In *Die Götter im Exil* (*The Gods in Exile*), originally published in 1853 in Germany, Heine offers us a grand, fantastical metaphor. Imagine, he says, the fates of the classical Greek and Roman gods as Christianity came into the ascendant. The temples where the gods lived were pulled down or converted into churches; there was no one to offer them wine or provide them with food – or indeed to love them. Being immortal, they couldn't be killed, but they were outlawed and had to go into hiding, put on disguises and find work. Zeus became a fisherman in Iceland; Bacchus, who always wanted to party, became an innkeeper, and Apollo, once the god of music and reason, had to take a job as a shepherd in Germany.

The most touching parts of the essay concern the exiled gods' search for understanding and appreciation: they long to be taken seriously and to be properly honoured. They're always trying to let people know they are still around and always getting into trouble with serious, respectable people.

Psychotherapy often, and with reason, wants to trace our current sufferings to the troubles of our early life, but perhaps there is as much to be learned from a loving engagement with our earlier happiness. If we're charmed by his story, we're perhaps being charmed by the idea of refinding the more carefree, less obedient, more joyous parts of ourselves. Heine's aim is to make us feel sympathy for the exiles, but he's really asking us to feel tenderness towards the parts of ourselves we've disowned in the name of maturity, and to bring them home.

Gisèle Freund, *Virginia Woolf,
London*, 1939

*The future, blissfully, will be
utterly indifferent to almost
everything we care about.*

Virginia Woolf,
How it Strikes a Contemporary, 1923

We don't obsess about it all the time, but at the back of our minds we fret about how the future will judge us. We might worry how we will answer the probing questions of our grandchildren regarding our conduct and attitudes; we are encouraged to place ourselves on 'the right side of history'. It's as if we have in mind a tribunal, to be established in the early decades of the 22nd century, that will sift through our lives and assign praise and blame.

Virginia Woolf would be a lovely person to talk to about this. Born in 1882 into an intellectually distinguished and well-to-do family, she was part of the Bloomsbury Group, who were really just her personal friends, but who went on to become a major force in English-language writing and publishing.

In particular it would be fun to ask her about this essay of hers, which was published on 5th April 1923 in the prestigious *Times Literary Supplement*, in which she wonders what the future will make of the culture of her time.

What's fascinating and helpful is how bizarre her worries are. She's very concerned that we, a hundred years in the future, will be troubled by, and contemptuous of, the standard of essay writing in the 1920s. It's hard to believe, but this is what she really thought we'd be asking about as the basis of our view of the 1920s. She wasn't wrong by a little: her vision of the concerns of the future now reads as imbecilic. We have to almost forcibly remind ourselves that Woolf was exceptionally intelligent and perceptive. And that's the point: however clever we are, our guesses about how the future will judge us are bound to be comically, absurdly wrong.

It was impossible for Woolf to imagine that we would not be urgently concerned about the decline (as she saw it) of prose style but would be much more engaged by the quantity of coal that was being burned to heat people's houses. For all we know, in another hundred years the priorities will be reversed: from a bunker on Mars an aesthete will be fretting about the use of metaphor in early 21st-century poetry and wondering why we, back on dreary Earth, were all so preoccupied by carbon.

We try so hard, we worry, but in the long run we haven't a clue how we'll be judged. Except for this: we love Virginia Woolf's boldness and honesty, we like her voice and her good intentions. The future won't care if we got it right or not, because we couldn't possibly have. But they still might admire our nice intentions.

Crowds at the Paris Motor Show in the
Grand Palais surround a Citroën DS-19
on display, October 1955

Everything is fascinating.

Roland Barthes,
Mythologies, 1957

Modern societies can seem disgustingly trivial. We put huge efforts into marketing brands of soap or making game shows; as civilisation collapses we're talking about makes of cars or lapping up celebrity gossip. Why can't we turn away from such things and focus on the real issues?

In 1957 the French philosopher Roland Barthes published a beautiful response to these frustrations: nothing is really trivial; the grandest themes are always being played out everywhere. Born in 1915 and often ill as a child, Barthes was outwardly very correct, neat and cautious. Intellectually he was obsessed with 'signs': when one thing stands for another. *Mythologies* is a series of essays on what the apparently banal objects of quotidian life really mean.

In one essay on cleaning products, for instance, he takes us into the supermarket: there's a detergent that promises to *eradicate* practically all germs. It's merely selling us a domestic fluid, but at the same time it is preaching and subtly normalising a vision of life: bad things must be destroyed; we know our enemy, who shall (and must) be removed by violent means. A rival product promises to clean deeply but *gently*: our enemies will still die, but this time engulfed in kindly foam; our troubles will, without fuss, simply be made to vanish. A battle between huge rival ideologies is being played out in packaging.

He was also very interested in the ways people talk about cars. The Citroën DS, featured on the cover of an early French edition of the book, was particularly prestigious at the time. 'Citroën' alludes to the owner as a plain 'citizen', but the name also suggests divine status, 'DS' sounding in French like *déesse*, meaning goddess. Thanks to an innovative system of suspension, the car has an especially 'smooth' ride; it seems to lift the driver above the road. Far from being a simple means of transport, it offers to solve a major conundrum of existence: how to be down to earth and yet nobly elevated at the same time. This elusive, mature condition, which was once the life goal of figures like Montaigne and Goethe, is now available to anyone who can stump up the purchase price.

Barthes is equally alert to the meaning of plastic toys for children, staged wrestling matches, magazine covers and the marketing of margarine, but the help he offers isn't tied to the particular things he finds so suggestive. What matters is the move he shows us how to make: what are the big, but covert, messages that ordinary things might be trying to send us?

The message might be a bit cynical: sparkling wine, Barthes argues, is so popular because it suggests 'sparkling conversation', even though the wine itself has no power to make us witty; we're being sold a beguiling falsehood. But there is no reason why a beautiful or hopeful message might not also be quietly transmitted: when we pop the cork we are paying homage to a lovely social vision, in the realisation of which we need all the support we can get.

Lucian Freud, *Sir Isaiah Berlin*, 1997

*Sometimes we are indecisive, muddled and
hesitant, not because we are weak, but
because we are thoughtful, alert and
intelligent.*

Isaiah Berlin,
Two Concepts of Liberty, 1958

There are times when we feel torn between different options. Should we leave a relationship that has many problems but is genuinely good in some ways and search out another, perhaps more independent, life? There is much to be said for staying, for appreciating what we have, for being loyal to someone even when things are difficult. And there's much to be said for discovering who we might become if we stepped away.

Or we really want to be devoted to our children and give them the best care and attention we can, but at the same time another part of us wants to press on with career opportunities that offer us the chance to use our abilities in very interesting and rewarding ways.

Or we might be unsure whether to stay in the city, with our friends, and immerse ourselves in all the metropolis offers or move to a quiet place in the country where life will be simpler and slower. Both have their appeal. We feel upset in part because we're haunted by the idea that there is a right decision in such cases, only we are too confused or too weak to find it and take it.

It's then that Berlin wants to invite us along to a talk. Born in Riga in 1909, Berlin lived in St Petersburg as a child, and was there when the Bolsheviks seized power in 1917; in his early teens he moved with his family to the UK. *Two Concepts* is the text of Berlin's inaugural lecture as Professor of Social and Political Theory at Oxford, delivered when he was approaching 50.

His core idea is that there are multiple *divergent* good things. It sounds rather abstract, but it has powerful practical consequences. What he means is that when we pursue one good thing we are automatically and inevitably moving away from *other* things that would also be good. In other words, we cannot possibly get all the good things. This is what it is to be free to choose. We are condemned to face a problem to which there is no perfect solution; there is only a choice about which things we will miss out on. Our fantasy is that freedom will make us happy, because then we can choose what we really want. The truth is that freedom brings a special kind of suffering because whatever we choose will be wrong in some way.

What's so sweet about Berlin's idea is that it's emphatically *impersonal*. He's pointing to a difficulty of existence that arises simply from the logic of choice. It's not our personal fault or weakness or stupidity that leaves us muddled and torn. This is a price we all have to pay, and a sorrow we all secretly share, for the privileges of being imaginative and of having options. In essence, he is dignifying our trouble.

Marlis Schwieger, *Anaïs Nin*, 1950

The book is dedicated to 'Sensitive Americans — may they create a sensitive America.' How, whether American or not, can we make a more sensitive world?

Anaïs Nin,
The Novel of the Future, 1968

We'd love to bludgeon people into being lovely, were it not the most self-defeating strategy of all time. So let's ask a tricky question: where, actually, does sensitivity come from? Can it be awoken in others? How might it be transmitted?

Some of the most interesting suggestions come from a writer whose outward story is frankly disturbing. Anaïs Nin was born in 1903 into a family of French, Cuban and American heritage. As a child she had an exceptionally complex relationship with her father (with whom she claimed to have had, in adult life, an affair). She was a flamenco dancer, she wrote pornographic novels, she trained and worked as a psychoanalyst; for some years she maintained two marriages (one in California and one in New York) without either partner knowing of the other.

Yet this picture of her life, which perhaps makes her existence seem extreme and unusual, is misleading. As she saw it, she was living out the unconscious dreamworld of normal people: She was utterly average – that is, crazy, on the inside. She was just (as she saw it) a little more frank in her actions than most. In her 60s she came to the tender, and quite possibly correct, view that societies become harsh, rather than sensitive, when they are afraid of, and hostile to, the ordinary but very strange-sounding material that circulates in the deeper regions of our imaginations.

Her programme for 'sensitising' America, and by extension the world, is announced in her vision of what novels ideally will be like in the future. They should report our 'dreams', that is:

ideas and images in the mind not under the command of reason. It is not necessarily an image or idea that we have during sleep. It is merely an idea or image which escapes the control of reasoning or logical or rational mind. So that 'dream' may include reverie, imagination, daydreaming, the visions and hallucinations under the influence of drugs – any experience which emerges from the realm of the subconscious.

People become insensitive (hard, cold, closed-minded) when they lose contact with the irrational, slightly mad, yet authentic parts of their nature. She was an early proponent of the idea that we are particularly harsh on the weaknesses of others that secretly appeal to us. But they feel they live in a world that will be unkind to the more sensitive and less constrained part of who they are and so they attack others to protect themselves. Those most urgently censorious of her bigamous marriages would be, she felt sure, those who were secretly attracted to such a possibility for themselves.

The novel of the future is the guide to exploring the things that tantalise but frighten us, and that can, if we explore them, make us kinder to and more understanding of others: the strangeness of others is only a variant of our own.

I make the acquaintance of Miss Mowcher.

'I make the acquaintance of Miss
Mowcher', illustration from Charles
Dickens, *The Personal History of David
Copperfield*, 1900

*Why we might need to feel greater
sympathy for those who don't seem to
deserve much.*

Martha Nussbaum,
'Steerforth's Arm' (from *Love's Knowledge*), 1990

One evening, the distinguished US philosopher Martha Nussbaum was reading Dickens' *David Copperfield* to her young daughter. But when they came to an important scene, Nussbaum was disturbed to see her daughter getting distressed.

The problem involved a character in the book called James Steerforth. As Nussbaum remembered from her earlier readings of the work, Steerforth is a reprobate. He is a young man with a great deal of charisma. He can be charming and sweet, but he's also rather snobbish. He doesn't consider the consequences of his actions, and he can be extremely selfish.

At a climactic moment in the story, Steerforth is shipwrecked and drowns in a brave but hopeless rescue attempt. His body is later dragged ashore and the titular David Copperfield weeps over his corpse. What disturbed Nussbaum was that her daughter, too, seemed ready to shed a tear. Didn't she realise this was poetic justice? Steerforth was bad and therefore unworthy of love.

Dickens himself seems to prefer another view: those who love Steerforth want to say he actually did no wrong, that he was misunderstood or misguided by unfortunate friends. He was loveable and therefore incapable of actual, deliberate wrong. But Nussbaum didn't like this either – obviously Steerforth really *did* behave badly a lot of the time.

The joy of the essay consists in the grave and grand attention Nussbaum pays to this passing moment as she read and as her daughter wept: from this tiny, intimate event she evolved a magnificent theory of the human condition.

Let's say, she suggests, that both she and her daughter are right. Steerforth is rather horrible and at the same time loveable; he is both properly adorable and genuinely to be condemned.

The beautiful expression of our full humanity is that we are committed to both these opposed views at the same time. We fully see the sin but we still love the sinner. We are torn apart: a part of us knows he was a kind of monster and a part of us feels immense sympathy. The temptation is to opt for one side or the other. But, Nussbaum argues, the real point is not to resolve this split but to recognise it as an inevitable element in a mature philosophy of life.

It is the position of the parent: *I will love my child whatever. I will never stop loving, even though they may, objectively, do wrong, which I acknowledge. I will be both loving and moral, which means I will suffer.*

Yet the ultimate meaning is about ourselves. To a degree, we are all Steerforth, with a mixture of merits and faults. We long for someone to bear with us: to say, 'I fully see the wrongs you have done, I'm under no illusions *and* I continue to love you.'

XI.
Fiction

Matthew Merian the Elder, *A Lion's Gratitude*, copper engraving from J.L. Gottfried, *Historische Chronica*, 1630

Wisdom made simple and memorable.

Aesop,
'Androcles and the Lion', 550 BCE

An unfortunate characteristic of human beings is that we tend, under pressure, to jettison our more careful and accurate insights. We know, for instance, that we should patiently discuss a point of disagreement, we should listen with an open mind, we should search reasonably for compromise and mutual accommodation. In reality, we get frustrated, we feel misunderstood, we panic, we raise our voice or storm off. It's as if, under pressure, we forget what is clear to us in our calmer moments. Ideally, we'd like a mechanism that kept the wiser insight more powerfully at the front of our minds for longer.

'Androcles and the Lion' is a story written precisely to provide this kind of therapy. Also known as 'The Shepherd and the Lion', it's attributed to Aesop, a perhaps purely legendary figure imagined by later scholars to have been a slave who gained his freedom and wandered the eastern end of the Mediterranean in the 6th century BCE, enchanting local rulers and the wider population with his short, pointed fables, in which animals always play a major part.

The tale of Androcles is straightforward. One day Androcles comes across a lion; the lion is roaring and looks terrifying, but Androcles eventually notices it has a large thorn embedded in its paw; he extracts the thorn and the lion becomes friendly. The story has been retold and embellished many times, but in its core version it is only a few lines long.

As guidance for interacting with actual lions it is, of course, absurd. If we are unlucky enough to be menaced by a lion it's most unlikely to have a thorn in its paw. If it does, the last thing we should attempt is to remove it ourselves.

The 'lion' in the story stands for a person: anyone who intimidates, bullies or just annoys us. The 'thorn' stands for a theory: it's the idea that *something* – which we can't see yet – is distressing this person, and their irritating or oppressive (or rude or brutish) behaviour is a symptom of their suffering. It's a generous and often well-targeted point. When we dig into the life history of unusually aggressive or very difficult individuals we can be almost sure to find some major 'thorn'. Their childhood left them deeply insecure, there was some emotionally devastating loss or they were over-exposed to intimidation or harsh demands, which they now enact on others. The benign, and reasonable, assumption is that they aren't intrinsically horrible; rather, something they didn't choose is causing them to behave horribly.

We won't know exactly what it is, and we may not be able to do anything to remove the thorn. But knowing it is there changes our reaction. Of course we don't like how this individual is behaving, but we can feel pity for them. We grasp that, at some level, they are in agony, even if they seem to hide it well.

We might still forget as the pressure mounts, but the core idea ('roaring is a symptom') has more chance of being heard when we need it.

Torii Kiyonaga, *Murasaki Shikibu*,
c. 1779–1789

*Counteracting the natural provincialism
of the soul.*

Murasaki Shikibu,
The Tale of Genji, 1000 CE

We are, unavoidably, creatures of our time and place. Our background and experience teaches us to regard certain ideas and values as natural and right, but our familiar province represents only a tiny, strange sliver of the full range of what can seem, or has felt, obvious to others.

The assumptions of here and now don't necessarily fit our needs. There are multiple versions of who we might be, given slightly different encouragement. Parts of who we are might feel more at home in other times and places. To immerse ourselves in a work from long ago isn't primarily a matter of academic research – disinterested curiosity about the oddity of long-vanished cultures – but a quest to find a proper home for some outcast fragment of ourselves.

We may be holding down respectable jobs, but there could be a potential pirate somewhere inside us, just as there might have been a potential tax accountant or special-needs teacher lurking in the soul of a 17th-century Algiers-based corsair. In other circumstances, we might have taken wholeheartedly to the Russian Orthodox Church or joined the Shining Path revolutionary army.

By sloughing off the prejudices of today, certain novels invite submerged parts of ourselves to the surface. *Genji Monogatari* (*The Tale of Genji*) was composed around 1000 CE by a lady-in-waiting at the imperial Japanese court who wrote under the name Murasaki Shikibu. It is mainly focused on the love lives of the highest-ranking courtiers and members of the imperial family. In this vast, intricate story, Genji, a minor son of an emperor, is held up as the ideal human being.

For much of the book, Genji is in his late teens and 20s, and his erotic exploits are described at great length. In this world, what makes him so admirable is that he knows how to conduct several simultaneous liaisons discreetly.

He's a hero, too, because he loves drinking parties, has remarkably fine taste in trousers and cloaks and walks more beautifully than any other man. Genji isn't a rebel or a counter-cultural figure, he's a great figure of the establishment.

But what really makes Genji so splendid, in the eyes of the novelist, is his poetic refinement. He is deeply responsive to the aesthetic details of landscape, to the effects of mist, frost, rain and sunshine. He's obsessed with flowers and associates each of his lovers with a particular kind of blossom. He is brilliant at adapting lines from classical poetry to hint at his sentiments, and the ability to continue a conversation in this allusive way is one of the things he most values in others. Genji, in effect, is something that can't exist today: he's a total cad and the most sensitive person in the world.

The Tale of Genji is *symbolic* in the sense that it symbolises an important kind of therapeutic reading. This may not be precisely the book for us, but we may need another book that promises the same *kind* of help: the offer of refuge for a currently homeless part of ourselves.

Suad al-Attar, *From a Thousand and One Nights 1*, 1984

One of the best things, paradoxically, about exciting books is that they aren't really all that exciting.

One Thousand and One Nights, 1775

We need entertainment. There are times when we rightly want distraction and a temporary escape from our preoccupations. But a tragic interplay of modern technology and market competition for attention means that tens of thousands of the cleverest and most creative people in the world are labouring so that we never want to stop looking at our screens. We have to prise ourselves away by an act of will and might regularly find ourselves at 2 a.m. unable to resist yet another episode. The root of the problem, and the thing that's being ruthlessly exploited, is that our brains are finely geared to respond to visual stories: they slip in effortlessly, even when we are, objectively, utterly exhausted and practically propping our eyes open. Of course, we regret it the next day.

It's not that writers haven't tried to make their books and stories as fascinating as possible. The symbolic representative of this ambition is the collection of traditional Middle Eastern and North African tales that were gradually assembled together over several centuries under the title *One Thousand and One Nights*.

The stories are framed by a gruesome situation: 'a wicked king' takes a new wife every evening only to have her executed in the morning. When he weds a young woman called Scheherazade she starts telling him a story but breaks off with the hint that an even more exciting part is still to come. To hear what happens next the king has to postpone her fate. The following night, Scheherazade continues the tale but again stops on the cusp of a new episode, so the king spares her life a second time. She keeps this up for, as the title suggests, 1,001 nights, until all thought of having her killed has long gone and the king realises he loves her.

The book works because so many of the tales – like the adventures of Sinbad the Sailor, and the stories of Aladdin and the magical lantern and Alibaba and the Forty Thieves – really are captivating and have been found thrilling by generations of people around the world.

So far, it sounds like it's a parallel to our inability to get ourselves off the sofa even though it's insanely late. But the difference is that this is a book: we are readers rather than viewers. Unlike watching a film, reading requires a concerted effort of will: we have to focus on each line and each word. As we get tired our heads droop, our eyes lose their place, the words drop out of focus. No matter how interesting the text, we simply can't go on. Our brains start to shut down and sleep overwhelms us.

This is why reading in bed at night is one of the nicest and most useful things: the right book is thrilling enough to tempt us to get between the sheets and follow the next instalment but before too long we're drifting off. And instead of launching into yet another too-late night at the screen we find we're falling asleep and setting ourselves up for a good tomorrow.

Illustration from Johann Wolfgang von
Goethe, *Wilhelm Meister's Apprenticeship*,
c. 1802

We need to make lots of mistakes.

Johann Wolfgang von Goethe, *Wilhelm Meister's Apprenticeship*, 1796

In certain moods, the story of our lives can feel like a shameful, horrifying sequence of errors. We chose the wrong friends, set out on the wrong career, married the wrong person and made the wrong financial choices. We desperately wish we could start life again and get it right this time.

In the 1790s, when he was writing *Wilhelm Meister* (and approaching 50), Goethe was having similar thoughts. He'd spent years as a high-level government bureaucrat in the German state of Weimar, but he'd accomplished little. His biggest project – reactivating a defunct state-owned silver mine – was a disaster. After fleeing many potential relationships, he'd recently got married and discovered, almost at once, that he'd made an insane choice.

Goethe wasn't an objective failure in life but, like the rest of us, he judged himself against what he would have been like if he hadn't made so many missteps: the people he'd needlessly alienated, the opportunities he'd let slip, the potentially great relationships he'd squandered, the good advice he'd rejected, the terrible advice he'd willingly embraced …

Wilhelm Meister is an exercise in self-therapy. It's the story of a young man, Wilhelm, who is almost comically prone to getting his life wrong. He grows up wanting to be a poet and hating the family business. Then, following a disastrous romance in which his beloved runs off with someone else, he decides all he cares about is commerce, but he's terrible at it. On a business trip he meets a bankrupt acting company and pours the family fortune into it, only to discover he has no idea how to manage a theatre. Every chapter recounts a new disaster of his own making.

The running joke in the story is that all the time Wilhelm is being watched by a deeply serious and immensely kindly group of philosophers who could step in at any moment and save him from his mistakes, *but they never do.*

When he eventually gets to know them, they explain: it is *only* through mistakes that anyone attains wisdom. To rob someone of their errors would be to rob them of their chance to grow. It's only pain and regret that ever pushes a particle of practical good sense into our poor brains.

In a key passage, Wilhelm is formally received into the clandestine committee of the wise and they offer him *their* candid confessions, all of which are the horrible stories of *their* absurd mistakes and stupid follies. To be an adult, Goethe is saying, is to realise that everyone has a secret history of endless idiocies. What makes someone wise isn't that they didn't make mistakes but precisely that they are interested in their errors. Indeed, if Goethe himself hadn't made so many blunders in *his* life, he could hardly have written this novel.

In our errors and misguided ideas we're not failing to live properly. We are participating deeply and genuinely in the only story available to us, or to anyone: the fascinating, moving and oddly magnificent tale of our failures.

Cassandra Austen, *Portrait of
Jane Austen*, c. 1810

*We can accept that others might
find us boring.*

Jane Austen,
Mansfield Park, 1814

Deep inside ourselves, we may come to the painful conclusion that we are boring. We don't do anything particularly adventurous and don't especially want to; we have few, if any, radical opinions; we're accommodating rather than headstrong; we live quiet, respectable and (as others might say) dull lives.

There is no sweeter friend we could have than Jane Austen. Born in 1775, she was almost the comic opposite of our idea of what a great writer is supposed to be like. She led a desperately uneventful life: her world was largely confined to her genteel but impoverished family circle; she never married and had only one brief, unhappy, romance; she was brisk, cheerful, neat, patient, polite and very careful with money. She never got into a rage and she never rebelled.

Mansfield Park, which she wrote in her late 30s towards the end of her short life, was published in 1814. It was her favourite among her own works, though it was ignored by reviewers and slow to sell, despite the promising reception of her earlier novels.

The central character, Fanny Price, is timid, uncomplaining, self-denying, hard-working and respectful of authority. She's not remotely beautiful – a fact that no adaptation of the book has dared to convey. She has no ambition. Yet she is, in Jane Austen's eyes, profoundly loveable. As a child, Fanny is adopted by her much grander and wealthier relatives and goes to live with them in their magnificent country house, Mansfield Park. To her worldly and elegant cousins she is a nobody and something of a killjoy. She isn't interested in excitement; she's not daring; she never gets carried away by the moment. Everyone turns against her for being, as they think, so tedious and limited.

Austen organises the story so that, eventually, everyone else comes to some kind of ruin or embarrassment. Only modest, shy, industrious Fanny emerges as an individual of honour and dignity. At the end, the nicest of her cousins realises he loves her, marries her and then happens to inherit the whole estate; Fanny is installed as the true mistress of the great house. The story can be seen as a meditation on the Christian idea that 'the meek shall inherit the earth'. It isn't a prediction. Austen doesn't think that modest, deeply honourable people usually end up in positions of power and responsibility; she just wishes they did.

The book is a restrained hymn sung in praise of those whose merits, while very real, are normally overlooked. While we may never fall in love with an awkward cousin who becomes heir to a substantial fortune, we may, as we live our unrecognised and not particularly well-rewarded lives, know that Jane Austen admires us and is quietly but warmly applauding from the sidelines.

Antoni Kozakiewicz, *Matthias, King of
Kings* in *Pan Tadeusz*, Book VI, 1879

*Nostalgia, though dismissed by many,
has much to teach us.*

Adam Mickiewicz,
Pan Tadeusz, 1834

Nostalgia rarely gets a good press. It feels like a sin against the present – and indeed the future – to pine for the past. We feel weird that our imaginations are so drawn to a time that has definitively gone, and we blame ourselves for looking backwards. But this tendency in our nature, which we feel required to deprecate, may actually be one of our greatest assets.

Adam Bernard Mickiewicz was born in 1798 into an upper-class but financially constrained Polish family. As a student at the University of Vilnius in the 1820s, he got involved in what was then considered radical politics and was forced into exile, from which he never returned. On his travels he met Hegel and Goethe, both of whom took a liking to him. He lived for years in Paris, but died in his late 50s in Constantinople. He'd gone there in the hope of fighting against the Russians in the Crimean War but died of cholera before he could reach the battlefront. He had wild hair and brooding looks but was immensely polite and charming.

Pan Tadeusz, widely regarded as the central work of Polish literature, is a long poem, subtitled 'A Tale of the Years 1811–1812'. It was published in 1834 in Paris, when Mickiewicz was in his mid-30s. The work is an epic distillation of his love for all that he had lost.

It tells the story of a student, Tadeusz, who comes home from university to the small ancestral estate far out in the country. (*Pan*, at the time, was a Polish title indicating membership of the lower nobility.) His extended family gets embroiled in an age-old property dispute with a neighbouring noble clan, which leads to an armed skirmish; he falls in love, goes hunting with his friends and attends a wonderful family feast.

What's moving is the expansive seriousness with which the past is evoked: even its troubles and difficulties were, in retrospect, delightful. In the final chapter we learn that, a few years later, when the world has changed, Tadeusz has become friends with his former enemy. The things that once set them at odds seem trivial; they shared *that time*. It's like the way in which, as we get older, we come to realise that we have more in common even with the people we hated in the past than we do with our younger contemporaries. They may have been bullies or timid conformists but they breathed the same air, they knew the same music. It turns out we share many ideas because they were assumptions of the epoch.

What we dismiss as nostalgia can be a grand meditation on the effects of time. Our differences are smaller than they seem at first. Gradually all our preoccupations will feel dated. They will be merged in the general outlook of the period. And we will long for the company of those who understand. When we love the past we are doing ourselves a great and central kindness: we are loving a part of ourselves that isn't appreciated in the present.

Illustration from Gustave Flaubert,
Madame Bovary, first serialised in *Revue
de Paris*, 1 October–15 December 1856

*For all its wonders, modern life drives
us slightly mad.*

Gustave Flaubert,
Madame Bovary, 1856

Serialised in the *Revue de Paris* in the autumn of 1856, *Madame Bovary*, Flaubert's novel, on which he'd been working obsessively for five years, was considered so scandalous that he was tried (and acquitted) on a charge of obscenity. However, when it was published as a two-volume book the following year it sold well and established Flaubert as a prominent writer.

Set in Normandy, where Flaubert was born and had lived for the first two decades of his life, the novel tells in highly realistic detail the story of the marriage of Emma, the pretty daughter of a dour but relatively prosperous farmer, and Charles Bovary, an ordinary, well-intentioned, not especially able and not particularly ambitious local doctor.

In the traditional history of French provincial life, this would have seemed like an ideal match. An Emma of former times may not have been especially excited by her husband, but she would have been proud of her entry, via marriage, into the professional class. She would have accepted her lot as the will of heaven, and she would no more have thought of trying to change it than of single-handedly changing the course of a river or the coastline of France.

But the novel is set in the 1850s, when the forces of modernity were beginning to work their way into the inner lives of people like Emma – and, eventually, people like us.

Emma's view of life has not been formed by her own direct experience, or by tradition or religion, but by Romantic novels. She believes that it is her destiny to enjoy a profound, soul-stirring, emotionally overwhelming feeling of love. When her husband almost inevitably fails to live up to this, she embarks on a series of affairs with men who find her exciting but don't truly return her deep passion.

In addition, Emma, in a newly liberal society, can imagine herself as the consort of a great aristocrat. She spends wildly on clothes in order to fit herself for the part, running up horrifying debts. Eventually everything collapses: the debts are called in, her lovers abandon her and Emma kills herself by taking arsenic.

It's not the specific details of the plot that speak to us (although Flaubert sets them out with extraordinary clarity and plausibility); it's rather that Emma, like us, is caught in an epoch of history. The modern world has released her into imaginative freedom. It tells her she could do and become and have anything she wants. Yet her life is actually immensely constrained, as every life necessarily is. Modernity tells her that she can rise in the world, that she will be happy if only she spends enough money and finds exactly the right partner – even though these possibilities are scarcely available to her in reality. She is maddened by the gap between what we are told we can have and what we can actually accomplish. And so, too often, are we.

Marcel Proust kneeling and holding
a tennis racket in front of Jeanne
Ponquet (the Gilberte de Proust) at
the tennis court of Boulevard Bineau
in Neuilly, 1892

We are our memories.

Marcel Proust,
In Search of Lost Time, 1913–1927

The horror of time seems to be that it is always flowing away. In certain moods, we can be transfixed by this appalling destiny: every day our future is shrinking. We don't know when our death will be; we can only be sure it's twenty-four hours closer than it was yesterday.

When we feel like this, Marcel Proust is longing for us to pick up one of the volumes of his novel *In Search of Lost Time*, because he wrote the books as a psychological balm for precisely this anxiety.

Proust was born in Paris in 1871 into a very successful, assimilated Jewish family; his father was an eminent doctor and a specialist in epidemiology.

Unable to settle to a normal career and having inherited enough to live on, in his 20s Marcel Proust became an ambitious socialite, obsessed with planning the perfect dinner party and anxious to be invited to the smartest, most fashionable events. He was a dandy and wrote a few charming essays.

In the latter part of his not very long life (he died, aged only 51, in 1922) he mainly stayed at home, often in bed, thinking and writing an immensely long, complex and beautiful novel, the single work of his maturity: *À la Recherche du Temps Perdu* (*In Search of Lost Time*), the last part of which was published posthumously.

Instead of gazing forward with dread, as we usually do, to the always shorter time we have left, Proust focuses on what has already happened to him – that is, on the always expanding time we've already had; the time that, we normally think, has gone.

The great secret Proust unlocked is that, rather than our lives diminishing, we become larger as the days pass. We grow to be what he calls 'giants in time'. If we give them enough loving attention, our memories are as real and substantial as the things that are happening now and that might happen in the future.

In regaining our past we're not merely reliving it as it was. We're now able to understand it more deeply than we could then. Baffling or frustrating experiences from long ago become much deeper and more meaningful when we relive them, imaginatively, from a loving adult perspective. A misunderstanding becomes poignant; a misstep becomes sweetly innocent.

The book is filled with the particularities of the life of the central character (who is clearly Proust himself) and goes into immense detail about the circumstances of existence in the late 19th and early 20th centuries. But all this is simply the way he shows us what we should, ourselves be doing. Like him, we should go on our own search for our lost time. He would have been saddened to think that decades later his admirers would seek out the places of his childhood rather than of their own. He ultimately wanted us to be our own Proust.

Giuseppe Tomasi di Lampedusa,
Il Gattopardo (The Leopard), cover of
edition published in 1958

*We don't let others know us fully because
we fear how they will judge us.*

Giuseppe Tomasi di Lampedusa,
The Leopard, 1958

There's something very appealing about the idea of being nonjudgemental. It means taking the time and trouble to really understand someone without feeling required to flatter or condemn; we simply come face to face with the reality of being that person. More intimately, we long that another could both know us deeply and accept us as we are.

Il Gattopardo (*The Leopard*) was published in 1958, shortly after the writer's death. It was the only major thing Giuseppe Tomasi di Lampedusa ever wrote. While he lived he only heard of its rejection by the various publishing houses to which he'd sent the manuscript – though it quickly became a huge, and very surprising, success.

Essentially the book is a detailed character study of one person: a middle-aged astronomer and mathematician called Fabrizio Corbera, who is also (like the author) a Sicilian aristocrat. The novel is mainly set in the 1860s, but its helpful message to us has nothing to do with Italian history.

The outer surface of Fabrizio is polished, elegant and charming. He is easy-going, polite, handsome and generous, but as we see him in greater detail he emerges as far from appealing: he's irritable, selfish, demanding, a little vain, withdrawn and proud – and he's recklessly running through the family money. But the novel takes us deeper: he's a human being facing the impossibly perplexing questions of existence. He knows he has wasted his life; he is overwhelmingly conscious that moment by moment he is approaching death; he loves his children but none of them, as adults, love him; he is devoted to his wife but is desperate for the erotic warmth she can't offer. Even his scientific brilliance (he has played an important role in mapping the asteroid belt between Mars and Jupiter) is revealed as a kind of narcotic: he plunges into precise observation and complex calculation to escape from the pains of daily existence, but it also signals his longing for 'the unreachable, the untouchable, the unknown'. At times he is immensely self-aware; at other points he unwittingly deceives himself.

The touching, helpful beauty of the book is that eventually Fabrizio is revealed as 'magnificently ordinary'. He is seen and described with an immensely kindly, loving detachment. In a central episode, at a party, he is at first depressed and disgusted by everyone around him: they are ugly, banal, greedy, stupid, shrill. Then 'his heart split open: he was them; he was made of the same material; nothing that is destined to die could deserve hatred'. No one would ever know he felt like this; they'd never guess he could be so tender and so moved.

No one will ever know us fully. But here, in the pages of this book, we can imagine being known through and through and treated with the honour we deserve, for all our stupid mistakes and petty failings. It's a book about one person, but it's meant to be a book about everyone. If we could see the whole story, our hearts would break with love and compassion.

Le petit Nicolas

Goscinny & Sempé

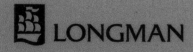

Goscinny & Sempé, *Le Petit Nicolas*,
cover of edition published in 1967

It's totally fine to be ordinary.

René Goscinny,
Le Petit Nicolas, 1960

We live in a world that tells us that we have to be special: to get noticed, to matter, to be liked or to be loved, we must have something remarkable to offer. It's an instinct massively supported by our broader culture. This has an obvious flaw: by definition, hardly anyone can be outstanding or special in ways that others will recognise and admire. As a consequence, we either have to assert our specialness in more desperate ways or we become cynical. In extreme moods, we view the world as mad and wicked, an arena in which only a small number of people ever get to be appreciated, and the entire edifice needs to be torn down before 'the little person' can be appreciated.

In the 1950s, the French writer René Goscinny, in collaboration with an illustrator of genius, Jean-Jacques Sempé, created one of the world's most useful fictional characters: a boy called 'little' Nicolas because he's the smallest in his class at school, who figured in a series of books. The grandeur of the project lies in the simple, sustained insistence that Nicolas is both lovely and completely ordinary. Nicolas has no special talents, he's not extraordinary in any way, but he is fundamentally good, even when, as quite often happens, he ends up causing a fair degree of chaos and consternation in the grown-up world.

Goscinny set out on a huge philosophical mission: he was trying to work out, and to show us, what human nature is. In the grand past, the positions had become polarised. In the 17th century (as we have seen), La Rochefoucauld had presented human nature as essentially vain and selfish, while the outstanding French thinker of the 18th century, Rousseau, had argued that human beings are essentially perfect: loving, kind and wise. Goscinny agreed with neither. Like us, probably, his Nicolas is neither a monster of self-interest nor an ideal being of generosity and candour. He's something else

entirely: he's out to have fun, he wants to be decent, he's intrigued (and sometimes bored) by other people; he's open to what other people might have to offer but devoted to his own point of view. He's sceptical of 'authority' that strikes him as silly, but not against the adult world in general. Nicolas is a fictional representation of human nature at its most normal: well-meaning, not much good at maths, friendly, irreverent, adventurous and occasionally quite naughty.

In the company of Nicolas, by liking him we can start to like our own imperfect, decent, muddled and well-intentioned selves more and find that, like him, we are already OK as we are.

XII.

Poetry

Dia al-Azzawi, *The Seven Golden Odes*
(The Mu'allaqat), 1978

Might one benefit from a little
judicious boasting?

The Mu'allaqat, 6th century CE

We are often told that boasting is unaccept-able. To brag about how great and special we are is to commit one of the most basic errors of social conduct.

This can be good advice – for other people. Self-aggrandisement, of course, is a vice in those whose egos are already inflated. But what if the problem is the other way around and our instinctive tendency is to think very badly of ourselves? In that case, a bit of self-praise might be an exercise in balancing the psychological books. Perhaps we concentrate on what is terrible about us and don't acknowledge the ways in which we are rather lovely.

A canon of pre-Islamic Arabic poetry, written before the advent of the Quran, *The Mu'allaqat* is still widely revered. The poems almost always include an 'encomium': a few stanzas in which the speaker explains why their camels are the best or their sword is the finest or why they are, personally, so fantastic.

We might suspect that their self-praise isn't particularly justified in realistic terms. Are their tents really more spacious than anyone else's? Are they actually so brave and wise?

These might not be productive questions. Inspired by the poems, we could, instead, ask what we might like to boast about. In what areas would we, despite our nice manners, want to de-clare our genius, in the manner of Oscar Wilde? Our assertions don't have to be literally correct; we can simply compensate for too much inter-nalised self-doubt.

We need to have an adjective for the opposite of boasting to describe our ingrained habit of self-condemnation. In effect, we say: 'My camels are horrible, my sword is useless, I am the opposite of fantastic.' But the criticism can be just as inaccurate as a boast. We are never as awful as we tell ourselves. What might feel like a boast might be, for us, a justified corrective swerve, a healthy impulse towards a more accurate picture of who we are.

Advice must depend on where we are starting from. With driving, obviously, the instruction 'turn second left' could be what leads us safely home or what sends us straight into a ditch. Equally 'big yourself up more' or 'be assertive about what's great about you' could be for some people the last thing they need to hear, but for us might be a guide to a more sane and less cruel assessment of our own real merits.

Yokoi Kinkoku, *The poet Basho with his most famous haiku 'An old pond – a frog jumps in'* from *Haikai Gunsen No Zu (Portraits of Haiku Poets)*, c. 1820

What seem like incidental, trivial things can become precious to us, if we pay them the right attention.

Matsuo Basho,
Haiku, c. 1644–1694

There's a bias in the human mind to dwell on the dramatic and the distinctive. We see this in the news, which tells us about the unusual things that have just happened, but also in the way we typically describe what occurs in our own lives: we focus on an argument that flared up at work, an unexpected message from an old friend, the new pepper grinder we bought. It's understandable but also unfortunate because most of life can seem, by contrast, hardly worth mentioning: our days slip by in a forgettable blur of sameness. But perhaps there's an antidote.

Living in Japan in what in the West is known as the 17th century, Matsuo Basho quickly found recognition and a livelihood as a poet. But he was so devoted to his art that public success meant little to him. At the height of his fame he withdrew into private life, he wandered in lonely places and was content to live, very modestly, in a series of small huts. He was – and still is – revered for his role in the development of an ultra-short kind of poetry, known as haiku, which is limited to a mere handful of words.

One of his most famous works of this kind goes like this:

Old pond,
frog jumps.
Splash!

At first, perhaps, it's baffling: it hardly says anything. So what if a frog jumped in a pond? Why should we care? But from this tiny observation we can expand the thought: we imagine the frog sitting very still, then the sudden burst of motion, the splash as it enters the water and then the ripples, which gradually die away. It might be a metaphor for a life: in the long span of time our life is a single leap; whatever impact we have will soon disappear and it will be as if we never existed.

A moment hardly worth mentioning ('I saw a frog, it jumped into a pond') becomes grandly significant because it is thoughtfully noticed.

The wider point thus has nothing to do with little creatures leaping into pools of water. Basho offers a model for how we might home in on the little details of our own lives. We become haiku poets to the extent that we highlight for ourselves the undramatic poignancy of certain moments. We're not trying to get the wording perfect, we're just sketching:

- a friend opened the fridge door and looked over their shoulder at us

- a bird gliding above the roof of an office building; the opalescent sky

- in the garden, weeding; the sound of a helicopter in the far distance

We don't have to immediately explain why these moments seem quietly meaningful. We could explore their resonance at great length and in doing so we are building the significance of otherwise fleeting, forgettable incidents of experience.

Our days are brimming with potential observations, suggestions, metaphors and thoughts. The full 'news' of an afternoon could take a lifetime to tell properly.

Scipio Moorhead, *Phillis Wheatley*,
frontispiece in Phillis Wheatley, *Poems
on Various Subjects, Religious and
Moral*, 1773

Why sunsets should be on the news.

Phillis Wheatley,
'A Hymn to the Evening', 1773

We often fail to appreciate what nature continually presents to us. We may never have looked carefully at the intricate beauty of a tree or observed for a whole fifteen minutes the shifting interaction of tide, sand and rock.

It's not so much that we are unobservant but that we lack a sense of how and why such things could matter. We don't deny they are nice, but we struggle to recognise their importance.

In writing 'A Hymn to the Evening', Phillis Wheatley tried to make us feel that certain natural sights have great moral and psychological consequence: around them we can discover who we are – or who we should be.

For Wheatley, a fine sunset is essentially a spiritual experience. We ideally lose ourselves in the contemplation of the thin, glowing bars of cloud; we are absorbed in the rich colours that 'through all the heav'ns are spread' while 'the west glories in the deepest red'.

For Wheatley the key thing is that the 'grand majesty' we see awakens in us a desire to participate. In those moments we want to live with the same lofty serenity. We want to be more like the evening sky. As does the evening sky, she writes, 'so may our breasts with ev'ry virtue glow'. Our more cynical intellectual understanding may tell us otherwise, but our emotions respond with awe and reverence.

Phillis Wheatley was born in West Africa. As a child, perhaps as young as 6, she was abducted by a local chieftain. She was subsequently sold through a chain of slave markets until she arrived in Boston in the USA.

Her new owners (the Wheatley family, whose name she was assigned) were struck by her intellect and treated her with generosity not typically shown to an enslaved person. They encouraged her to write poetry, eventually sending her to London in the company of their eldest son. In London, her poems were published to great acclaim, her book was bought by the great and the good, and she became a literary star.

On returning to the USA, Wheatley was liberated, married a freedman and then, under circumstances that are unclear, died in her early 30s.

Wheatley wanted us to love what she loved and to feel, as she did, the noble simplicity of the evening sky. In her mind, the point of art and poetry was to ennoble and calm us; she wanted to become, and wanted us to become, more serene and loftier in outlook. Normally, we are endlessly encouraged to contemplate our grievances. By contrast, Wheatley, who had many very real grievances, wanted to forget them and to merge herself with the beauty and dignity of nature.

Wheatley stands for an aspect of our own nature in which, too often, we lose faith. We're as responsive to the glow of evening as she was, but, unlike her, we don't build this into the core of our view of the human condition. The sunset is never on the news or in political journals, so we forget that the emotions it incites might be important. Phillis Wheatley asks us to correct our scale of values.

Charles Pierre Baudelaire, *Jeanne Duval*,
with an inscription to Paul Chenavard
c. 1862. Jeanne Duval was Baudelaire's
mistress and inspired the 'Venus Noire'
section of *The Flowers of Evil*

*Who can we turn to when we're revolted
by ourselves?*

Charles Baudelaire,
The Flowers of Evil, 1857

One of the odder capacities of humans is the ability we possess to be disgusted at ourselves. We get drunk; we waste money on frivolities; we spend days lying on the sofa looking at the ceiling; we squander a sunny afternoon feeling bored and resentful; we get excited by idiotic erotic scenarios; we show off and then wish we hadn't; we gorge at a feast, then look in the mirror; we fantasise about limitless luxury, then read an article about people living in squalor. We want to weep at our own monstrosity.

In such moods of self-disgust, we might discover the friend we need in the 19th-century French poet Charles Baudelaire. He was born in Paris in 1821, and his father, a high-ranking public official, died when he was very young. When he came of age, Baudelaire inherited a largish fortune, but he was so irresponsible that his family intervened, putting his money in a trust to stop him squandering it, which meant that he lived his whole adult life short of funds.

For more than a decade, from his early 20s, Baudelaire worked on a series of poems that were eventually given the collective title *Les Fleurs du Mal* (*The Flowers of Evil*), first published in Paris in 1857. By 'evil' he means the things that we feel we're not supposed to do but secretly want to. His own 'evils' were taking drugs, spending money he didn't have on beautiful clothes, staying in bed all day when he should have been writing, going to lowlife drinking dens and relishing the failures and disgraces of other people.

In the opening poem, 'To the Reader', he speaks directly to us as individuals. He accuses us of 'folly, error, sin, avarice'; he calls us 'filthy' and 'sordid'; he knows we're weak; we wish to change but don't; we pretend to be respectable and decent but know, deep down, that we're not. Finally, he produces one of the great lines of poetry:

Hypocrite lecteur, – mon semblable, – mon frère!

Reader you are a hypocrite, – you are like me, – you are my brother!

Or, indeed, sister. Our capacity to be ashamed of our actions and desires isn't what separates us from the rest of humanity, it's part of what brings us into the human community of fellow sufferers. Our hidden 'evils' could actually be the foundation of closeness, because so many others are, like us, secretly lamenting their own nature.

In a later poem in the collection, Baudelaire invites us to be braver:

*Donnez-moi la force et le courage
De contempler mon coeur et mon corps
sans dégoût*

*Give me the strength and the courage
to look, without disgust, at my own soul
and my own body.*

We did not invent the human condition. We didn't decide, stupidly, to be creatures whose desires are stronger than their reason; this is simply the kind of being we are. We're not supposed to be angelic, we're just designed to be what we are: like him, fascinating, broken, strange and really rather normal.

Augustus Leopold Egg, *Past and Present,
No. 3*, 1858

*Our sadness is not merely that we
have messed up or made mistakes, but
that in doing so we have forfeited
any claim on the kindness and
understanding of others.*

Francis Thompson,
'In No Strange Land', 1907

We all mess up our lives, but few people mess up more overtly than the 19th-century English poet Francis Thompson. Born in 1859 in the north of England, he was expected to follow his father's path as a successful medical practitioner. He dutifully spent his 20s at medical school, but rather than enter into practice he tried to live as a poet. Making no money, he made his way to London. He worked for a shoe repairer; he sold matches on street corners; he begged strangers for money; he slept under bridges; he became addicted to opium.

His finest poem was written in this period, though it was not published until many years later. It opens with the mood of his despair:

When so sad, thou canst not sadder.

It sometimes feels like this: our own wickedness has cut us off from tenderness, dignity and love; these are things we no longer deserve.

Thompson later said that he owed his life to a female prostitute who befriended him when he was on the verge of ending his own life. She was a complete outcast from respectability, degraded and in difficulty, but she gave more real kindness to him than anyone. In the poem he puts it metaphorically:

The angels keep their ancient places
But touch a stone you start a wing

The undeserved, loving kindness of another is there, in the least expected place. Behind the stone that seems so unresponsive, hard and indifferent is hidden a huge depth of tenderness. He's speaking of her but also of himself: who, seeing him in rags lurking under a railway bridge, would think he was incubating in his mind some of the most beautiful lines ever written in the English language? And he's speaking, too, of us: we may become stony on the outside (the world makes us harden our skins), but inside, somewhere, every particle of tenderness remains, waiting to be discovered.

Her, his, our hidden delicacy remains alive within; the sensitivity a passerby would never suspect, the depth of emotion, the longing for redemption, his feeling for sunlight reflecting on the river, his pathos for his fellow sufferers. All that we have ever loved and cared for is still active:

O world invisible, we view thee,
O world intangible, we touch thee,
O world unknowable, we know thee

We are creatures who, from failure, reach out to beauty and goodness. Unloveable, we crave love; confused, we seek the truth.

And he holds out the sweetest image of redemption:

Jacob's ladder
Pitched between heaven and
Charing Cross.

Charing Cross was the place of his shame, where he lived for years on the streets. A ladder has a lowest rung. Wherever the top may be we don't have to jump there directly; we need only take one tiny, almost bearable, step.

Thompson is so good for us because he knows the worst and darkest times; he wants to love the unbearable versions of who we are and to be by our sides when we think we are utterly alone.

Rabindranath Tagore, 1930s

Our idealism doesn't have to make us impatiently furious with the way the world is.

Rabindranath Tagore, 'Where The Mind Is Without Fear', 1910

What is the therapy for idealism? Does it even need one? The pain is that the more beautiful our social vision, the more appalled we are by what actually transpires in the world. But the source of the anguish needn't be the vision itself, which may be exceptionally wise and good. Rather the problem is to do with anticipation: how soon do we expect this to happen and what steps do we imagine will be required to bring about the universal perfection we long for?

We can focus this therapeutic idea on a poem by Rabindranath Tagore. Tagore was born in 1861 in Kolkata, into a princely and cultivated Hindu family. Well educated, he excelled in every area, physical, artistic and intellectual; he travelled the world, met everyone and was very handsome. In 1913 he won the Nobel Prize for Literature. Politically he supported Indian independence, though British rule ended only in 1947, six years after his death.

Around 1900 he wrote a characteristically hopeful, forward-looking poem, which he himself translated into English a decade later:

Where the mind is without fear and the head is held high
Where knowledge is free
Where the world has not been broken up into fragments
By narrow domestic walls
Where words come out from the depth of truth
Where tireless striving stretches its arms towards perfection
Where the clear stream of reason has not lost its way
Into the dreary desert sand of dead habit
Where the mind is led forward by thee
Into ever-widening thought and action
Into that heaven of freedom, my Father,
let my country awake.

It's a delightful, inspiring picture of how people, a nation and the world could be. Who wouldn't want to live somewhere where politicians' 'words come out from the depth of truth' or where communal life is guided by 'the clear stream of reason'? We're not wrong to want that. But does this good hope make us miserable or buoy us up?

It depends on how soon and how easily we expect such an awakening to occur. Anyone who imagined that a nation's transition to independence would quickly and automatically bring about such a utopia would be disappointed. But Tagore himself didn't assume this. Independence might be a good step, but it couldn't on its own make an irrational person reasonable or counteract the power of habit. He believed that only a complete reform of education (which he knew was unlikely to occur on the necessary, vast scale) could set the collective mind free. He set up a model school to show what such an education would look like, but it was just one school.

The therapy for idealism doesn't involve getting talked out of our ultimate hopes. What Tagore stands for is idealism of ends plus realism about means and time. We love the vision yet, at the same time, fully recognise and understand the obstacles to it. We should never be asked to abandon our ideals, only to adjust our time frame.

Apkar Retian, *C.P. Cavafy*, undated

Why it might be better not to settle down.

C.P. Cavafy, 'Ithaka', 1911

We spend much of our lives trying to fulfil our distant ambitions, wanting to create the circumstances in which, finally, we'll be happy. We'll have worked everything out, organised our way of life and, finally, we'll be happy. It's an enchanting idea but, ironically, it means that most of the time we're restless because we're not there yet. The present is just the tedious, dreary period we have to get through until, in the future, we can relax and enjoy ourselves.

The unexpected companion we perhaps need to ease our frustration is a bespectacled, Greek-speaking, middle-ranking civil servant: Constantine Cavafy, who was born in Alexandria in 1863. He often felt displaced; he lived almost all his life in Egypt but thought of himself as a citizen of Byzantium, once the capital of the Eastern Roman Empire.

Cavafy only hit his creative stride in his 40s and published little during his lifetime, held back by anxiety that the overtly homoerotic themes he often wanted to explore would be met only with condemnation.

The poem that does most to help us is entitled 'Ithaka'. Technically, the island of Ithaca was the home of the legendary Greek hero Ulysses, to which he spent ten adventurous years returning after the fall of Troy. But here it signals whatever we imagine our destination in life to be. It's the image we have in our heads of the distant time when we'll be able to live properly – once we've found a partner or bought a house or secured a divorce or made a fortune or retired. Cavafy doesn't want to help us get there more quickly; instead he wants to delay arrival for as long as possible.

As you set out for Ithaka
hope your road is a long one

Then he invokes what he calls 'harbours'.

May there be many summer mornings
when, with what pleasure, what joy,
you enter harbors you're seeing for the
first time

These, emphatically, are not our destination: they are the places and things, people and experiences we encounter precisely because we're not home yet, and that won't be available to us any longer when we finally get there.

His ideal is that when we arrive at our home we'll find that it is 'poor'; it has little to offer us.

Ithaka gave you the marvelous journey.
Without her you wouldn't have set out.
She has nothing left to give you now.
And if you find her poor, Ithaka won't
have fooled you.
Wise as you will have become.

If we live this way – with a warm sense of appreciation, with a sense of adventure, with a willingness to explore byways – our destination, when we get there, won't be the big fulfilment we once expected it to be. We'll have found our fulfilment along the way. It won't be what we find at the end that pleases us, so much as what we bring with us. It won't be marriage, making money or retiring that in itself is so great; what will matter is what we have discovered in ourselves before we reached these destinations.

Thomas Sturge Moore, front cover of W.B.
Yeats, *The Tower*, 1928

*How can we contain our growing anxiety
about getting old?*

William Butler Yeats, 'Sailing to Byzantium', 1928

People have always worried about death, but in modern times we have an additional psychological burden pressing down on us: our society is obsessed by, and celebratory of, youth.

William Butler Yeats, born in 1865, came from a cultivated and creative Anglo-Irish family; his father and younger brother were both distinguished painters. Even in his lifetime he was successful as a poet; aged 58 he was awarded the Nobel Prize for Literature. It was around this time he wrote this poem. It's not very long, only thirty-something lines. It opens with a frank declaration of our fear: wherever we are:

... is no country for old men. ...

An aged man is but a paltry thing,
A tattered coat upon a stick

To age is to be brushed aside, to become conspicuously pitiful. We become identified with the stupid failures of our bodies: a bad knee defines us in the eyes of the young. It's cruel, but in a way perhaps they are right. Who we really are – our ideas, loves, insights, personality – is indeed:

fastened to a dying animal

We may try to compete, we diet and exercise and seek ways to disguise our wrinkles, but it's hopeless. We'll secretly absorb the harsh condemnation, unless we adopt a very different approach. That is:

... unless
Soul clap its hands and sing, and louder sing
For every tatter in its mortal dress

We have to focus instead on what is inside us; we have to esteem the soul more every time the body lets us down. We abandon looking svelte and having glowing skin and turn our attention to:

Monuments of unageing intellect

We turn, that is, to the things that do not ask how old we are, or whether our toenails are in perfect condition or how much our skin might be sagging, but that instead want us to love the beauty and depth of an idea. Ideas have an entirely different history. What was wise in Plato or Confucius, in Ibn Khaldun or Montaigne, is wise today. It doesn't change with fashion. They are the singing masters of the soul.

And, as the young in turn age (as they think they won't), they will realise this too.

Yeats never went to the real city of Byzantium (or Istanbul) on the shores of the Bosporus, and that doesn't matter. He's not really thinking about a physical place. 'Byzantium' is his poetic name for the imagined place where wisdom and eternity are properly venerated, where getting old isn't the disaster we're told it must be. It's the place we can go to in our own imaginations, with him and with, ideally, some nice books and a friend or two.

W.H. Auden reading on the veranda, 1940s

Everyone we love will be difficult.

W.H. Auden,
'Lullaby', 1937

At first, everyone we fall in love with seems perfect. But as we get to know them more fully we discover their faults. They might have a mean side; they can be delightful and then, suddenly, hurtful; perhaps they are controlling or lazy or prone to sulks or to flirting with people we can't stand. At the same time, the closeness means they too will see our faults, which are many. The paradox of love seems to be that it allows us to see each other accurately and then, when we do, we stop loving.

A beautiful, redemptive response can be found in the work of W.H. Auden. Born in 1907, in the north of England, onto the lowest rungs of the upper-middle class, Auden embraced his homosexuality early and while a student at Oxford had a passionate relationship with fellow poet Stephen Spender.

If sentimentality is the denial of real troubles in favour of a comforting surface, Auden is the least sentimental of poets. The help he offers is his conviction that love can still flourish despite our clear-eyed awareness of all that standardly goes wrong in life.

'Lullaby' imagines the kind but very honest thoughts we might have as our lover lies by our side: I know you are human; I don't have faith in your perfection; I know, as a certainty, that we will let each other down. I know my beloved is mortal and guilty, but also beautiful, not because we are deluded into imagining they are perfect but because their troubles, sorrows, inner conflicts and worries move us so deeply. We love them not because we imagine them noble and whole; it's their brokenness that touches us.

We wish them so well. Auden gives us the tenderest words for what we want for them.

We are human and therefore 'crooked' – that is, made out of trauma, neuroses, desire and confusion. The only love we can give is human love, mixed with selfishness and misunderstanding. And that is all they can give us in return.

Auden's most beautiful insight is that we love each other because we are both damaged creatures. In another poem, closely related to this one, he imagines a central commandment of life: to love your 'crooked' neighbour with your own 'crooked' heart.

It's our sorrow and shame in ourselves that moves us to such compassion and tenderness for the other in their troubles. In our imperfection we can love our beloved for, not despite, their failings.

Paul M. Smith, *Joan Armatrading*, 1983

In praise of mishearing a line
of poetry.

Joan Armatrading,
'Heaven', 1983

In the past, much poetry was conveyed orally, often in song. The absence of a written text at times leads to a rather sweet issue of mishearing what was being said.

In a lovely essay from the 1950s, the US journalist Sylvia Wright confessed to having confused a line in a traditional Scottish poem her mother used to recite. On the page, the words read:

> *They have slain the earl of Murray*
> *And laid him on the green*

But Sylvia always thought her mother was saying:

> *They have slain the earl of Murray*
> *And Lady Mondegreen.*

She inadvertently introduced a new character and added a new dimension of romantic tragedy to the poem.

We tend to be a little stern around the misinterpretation of works of literature, but that is to neglect its creative potential.

The issue can be brought into focus via the lines of a great modern poem: the lyrics to the song 'Heaven', released in 1983 by British singer Joan Armatrading. She recounts her amazement and delight in discovering that another person can love her. In the moving chorus, she hopes to offer something in return. She sings that she wants to be the sunshine when someone is down.

It expresses the desire to cheer up the other person, to lift them out of their troubles with a sense of fun and lightness of being.

But the way the song is sung, as the chorus rises, leaves open a Mondegreen mishearing of the line. Joan Armatrading might actually be singing:

And I wanna be there sometime when you're down

It's a tiny shift in the stress on certain syllables; almost nothing in terms of sound. Yet the meaning of being there, sometimes, when you're down is quite different from wanting to be the sunshine.

The second, imagined, version is saying something like: 'I know you get down sometimes, and I know that you generally want to keep that hidden, but I would like to be there with you when you are sad and lonely. I don't know that I can help you, I don't know if I can cheer you up, but I want to be your companion when you are troubled. I want to be by your side and cry with you, and hold you. I love you not only because of your strengths and merits but because I am so moved by your vulnerability and self-doubt. I won't give up on you when you show me, and let me into, your sadness.'

'Sometime' is, perhaps, immensely important. It's not saying, 'I want to go low every time you do,' only that 'I want to truly know and understand that part of you. I want to be the loving witness of your broken self – but not all the time. Let me in occasionally, please.'

Our mishearings can be some of our most creative moments.

Epilogue:
The Promise of
A Book

Raymond Auguste Quinsac Monvoisin,
Telemachus and Eucharis, 1824

*The ideal book would be written by a
genius exclusively for us.*

François Fénelon,
The Adventures of Telemachus, 1699

We might approach a book with great hope. We've heard good things about it; it's going to solve our great problem; it's going to be truly, perfectly wonderful. And then we read it and it doesn't and isn't. What is this ordinary disappointment really telling us?

Between 1693–1694, one of the most prominent intellectuals in France (whose full name was François de Salignac de la Mothe-Fénelon) wrote perhaps the oddest book of all time. He was, at the time, engaged to coach a 13-year-old boy called Louis, who happened to be in the direct line of succession to the French throne and could therefore be expected, in those days, to become the most powerful person in the most powerful nation on earth.

Understandably, Fénelon wrote this book with one single, very pressing aim in mind: to shape the boy's outlook and character as benignly yet firmly as possible before his personality was unleashed on the entire world. Actually, little Louis was an inattentive student and Fénelon had to adjust the narrative to the most precise details of the boy's interests.

In *Les Aventures de Télémaque* (*The Adventures of Telemachus*), Fénelon casts his royal pupil as a classical hero – the son of Odysseus – not so much to flatter him but because the adventurous story of the *Odyssey*, filled with drama and adventure, was one of the rare books that Louis liked. In his adventures in the book, the young Louis-Telemaque is always meeting perfectly tailored reflections on his own life. Louis had just had a tearful break-up with a lovely young lady-in-waiting, so Telemaque falls in love with a beautiful dryad of the forest and gets his heart broken too. Now Fénelon can say to the fictitious Telemaque all the serious and helpful things he longs to say about adolescent romance that would be rejected by the real-life Louis.

In every chapter, little Louis (as the only reader) is confronted by issues that arise naturally in the career of a king: how to earn rather than just demand respect; how to frame the responsibilities of government; how to honour the legacy of his royal ancestors without repeating their errors of policy.

The charm of the book is that it implies what all books should be like. We should feel we are the central figure; that every idea has been designed specifically to address a current need in our lives or a future need in our careers.

In an explicit sense, this can never be: no huge figure of our times is going to study our private lives and devote their best years to teasing out how we, as precisely the individuals we are, should deal with our marriage, our job or our attitude to our wider family. Yet Fénelon tells us something enticing: this is where literature belongs. We can't commission someone else to write the book we most want and need – it's the book we have to write ourselves. All the books we read are, perhaps, at best offering paragraphs, themes, chapter titles and telling phrases.

The book of our life won't be written by
a genius; it will be written by us –
but it can be written with the help of
the wisest and most intelligent people
of all time.

The Journal

The single most important book in our therapeutic library – and indeed in the whole world – is one that hasn't yet been finished (and very probably will never be published): our own journal.

If we ask, ultimately, what we read for, it is to furnish our own minds with ideas. The knowledge, insights, characters and attitudes we encounter in books get accumulated in us; they form the private mental culture through which we interpret and understand our lives.

The things that happen to us, and the things we do, have no definite, fixed meaning in themselves: their significance depends on what we think about them. A trip to the supermarket could be a boring routine or an adventure in the observation of others. It could be a moment when we are astounded by modern convenience (as a medieval Russian peasant would be), or when we reflect on what it tells us about our society and its priorities. We might, in glancing at a particular make of biscuits, reconnect with our childhood; we may wonder what will be on the shelves in twenty years' time. What we *make* of a supermarket, or of anything, depends on what is going on in our heads. What is going on in our heads depends on what's in them already.

We said hello to someone briefly in the street; we woke in the middle of the night and looked out of the window at the moon; we meant to send a message to our mother but put it off. Whether these are banal, annoying, fascinating or noble experiences comes from us; it depends on how we interpret them.

This extends across the whole of life – what someone said to us when we were 6, where we went on holiday as an adolescent, where we happen to live, the kind of work we have, the relationship we are in or have been in; we are always interpreting. What we think and feel about who we are is a result of all these interpretations. To put it boldly, we are our thoughts.

The books we need are the ones that help us with this life-defining task. They're our guides for the interpretation of experience. In the right company, a setback is interesting and bearable. It is part of what draws us together: a theme of friendship, a source of insight, a universal moment. (In the wrong company, we're a loser.) In the right book company, we can delight in anything: sunshine falling in the late evening on an asphalt pavement; the beginnings of a smile on the face of someone whose respect we thought we'd lost; the realisation that we love someone more than we'll ever be able to convey to them.

In the best books, all this is met with open arms and recognition. Our best books say: 'You too?' They want us to bring the lonely, awkward and beautiful parts of who we are into orbit. We need them because they understand; they want us because we understand.

But books, however attuned to our secret needs, can only help; after reading, we have to apply.

At its core, a journal is the place where we attempt to use what we have read in the service of self-discovery. In our journal, we can take inspiration from spending time with Proust and Dante. We're not alone: our library is a set of voices we can employ as prompts and interlocutors. Collectively, they hold us when we are frightened; they whisper encouragement and commiseration; they share our sorrows and our times of shame and confusion; they weep with us; they entice our braver selves; they want everything good for us, while knowing how hard it is to be alive. They cluster around us, willing us on in an undertaking that they cannot perform for us but for which they love us: the attempt to tell the strangest, most confusing and most important story ever – that of our own lives.

List of Illustrations

p. 48   John Ruskin, *The Northern Arch of the West Entrance of Amiens Cathedral*, 17–18 May or 23 September 1856. Ashmolean Museum, University of Oxford. Photo © Ashmolean Museum, University of Oxford/Heritage Image Partnership Ltd/Alamy Stock Photo

p. 50   Jilly Cooper, *Riders* (London: Corgi, 1986). Originally published in the UK by Arlington Books Ltd, 1985

p. 54   Ibn Khaldun, *Al-Muqqadimah*, 15th century. British Library, London. Photo © British Library Board. All Rights Reserved/Bridgeman Images

p. 56   Mwana Kupona, a page from *Utenzi wa Hirqal*, a Swahili poem written in Arabic script, 1810–1860. SOAS Library, London (ref. MS 45022)

p. 58   Henrietta E. Marshall, *Scotland's Story: A History of Scotland for Boys and Girls*, London: T.C. & E.C. Jack, 1907. The New York Public Library. Photo: The New York Public Library Digital Collections

p. 60   Frances Partridge, *Dora Carrington, Saxon Arnold Sydney-Turner, Ralph Partridge and Lytton Strachey*, 1926–1927. National Portrait Gallery, London (NPG x13137). Photo © National Portrait Gallery, London

p. 64   Front cover of *The Rime of the Ancient Mariner* (first published in 1798) by Samuel Taylor Coleridge, published by Harrap, 1910. Mary Evans Picture Library

p. 66   Léon Brunschvicg, *Héritage de mots, Héritage d'Idées* (Presses Universitaires de France: Paris, 1950)

p. 70   *Krishna and Arjuna on a chariot*, from the *Mahabharata*, India, 18th–19th century. Ink on paper, 9.7 x 15.7 cm. National Museum of Asian Art, Smithsonian Institution, Freer Collection, Gift of Charles Lang Freer, F1907.627

p. 72   Kano Seisen-in Osanobu, *Portrait of So'o (Confucius)*, first half of the 19th century. Ink on paper, 151.4 x 82.3 cm. National Museum of Asian Art, Smithsonian Institution, Freer Collection, Purchase – Charles Lang Freer Endowment, F1981.18

p. 74   Rembrandt, *Christ Preaching (La Petite Tombe)*, c. 1657. Etching, engraving and drypoint; first of two states, 15.8 x 21 cm. Metropolitan Museum of Art, New York, H.O. Havemeyer Collection, Bequest of Mrs H.O. Havemeyer, 1929, Acc. 29.107.18

p. 76   Two pages from the Quran, Islamic School, 17th century. Musée Condé, Chantilly. Photo © Musée Condé, Chantilly/Bridgeman Images

p. 78   Joseph Mallord William Turner, *The Golden Bough*, exhibited 1834. Oil on canvas, 104.1 x 163.8 cm. Tate, London. Presented by Robert Vernon, 1847. Photo Tate, London

p. 82   Théodore Chassériau, *François VI, duc de la Rochefoucauld*, 1836. Oil on canvas, 73 x 57 cm. Chateaux de Versailles et de Trianon, Versailles. Photo © RMN-Grand Palais (Château de Versailles)/Daniel Arnaudet/Gérard Blot/Dist. Photo SCALA, Florence

p. 84   Silvestro Valeri, *Portrait of Stendhal*, 1835–1836. Photo: Alain Le Toquin/akg-images

p. 86   Sigmund Freud at his desk, Maresfield Gardens, Hampstead, c. 1938. Photo akg-images

p. 88   Richmal Crompton, *Just William's Luck*, published by George Newnes, 1948. Mary Evans Picture Library

p. 90   Dale Carnegie, *How to Win Friends and Influence People*, first published 1936. This edition published by The World's Work (1913) Ltd, Kingswood, Surrey

p. 92   Anna Freud at her desk in Berggasse 19, Vienna, c. 1920. Photo brandstaetter images/akg-images

p. 94   Edouard de Pomiane, *Cooking in Ten Minutes*, first published by Éditions Paul Martial in 1930 as *La cuisine en dix minutes*; first published in Britain by Bruno Cassirer in 1948; this edition dates from 1957

p. 96   Merze Tate with her bike at Oxford University, c. 1932. Courtesy of the Western Michigan University Archives and Regional History Collections

p. 98   Ingrid Vang Nyman, illustration of Pippi Longstocking. © The Astrid Lindgren Company™

p. 100   A drawing of Melanie Klein by one of her child patients, 1926. Wellcome Trust (PP/KLE/B.16), London. By permission of the Melanie Klein Trust

p. 102   Mark Gerson, *Donald Winnicott*, July 1963. Photo © Mark Gerson Photography. All rights reserved 2023/Bridgeman Images

p. 104   Onjali Raúf, *The Boy at the back of the Class* (London: Orion, 2018)

p. 108   Katsushika Hokusai, *Young Woman Reading 'The Pillow Book (Makura no Sōshi)'*, 1822. Colour woodblock print, 21.7 x 18.9 cm. Art Institute of Chicago, Clarence Buckingham Collection, 1928.1132

p. 110   Wittgenstein's cabin, Sognefjord, near Skjolden, Norway, 2019. Photo © Jon Bolstad

p. 112   Frederick Douglass in his Cedar Hill library, c. 1885. Photo Moorland-Spingarn Collection, Howard University Library

p. 114   Elizabeth Grant Smith, *Memoirs of a Highland lady; the autobiography of Elizabeth Grant of Rothiemurchus, afterwards Mrs. Smith of Baltiboys, 1797-1830* (London: J. Murray, 1911)

p. 116   E.O. Hoppé, *Halide Edib Adivar*, 1927. © E.O. Hoppe Estate Collection/Curatorial Inc.

p. 118   Malcolm X reading stories about himself in a pile of newspapers, c. 1963. Photo: Three Lions/Hulton Archive/Getty Images

p. 122   Benedict Anderson, *Imagined Communities* (London: Verso Editions and NLB, 1983)

p. 124   Kazuo Ishiguro, *An Artist of the Floating World* (London: Faber and Faber, 1986); paperback edition published 1987

p. 126   Gerhard Richter, *Grey*, 1974. Oil on canvas, 250.5 x 195.1 x 4 cm. Tate, London. Photo: Tate, London. © Gerhard Richter 2023 (0148)

p. 128   Earth over the horizon of the Moon, taken during the Apollo 8 mission, December 1968. Photo JSC/NASA

p. 130   Lossapardo, illustration for 'Notes on Grief' by Chimamanda Ngozi Adichie, published in *The New Yorker*, 2020. Copyright Lossapardo

p. 134   Antonio Maria Crespi (known as Bustino), *Portrait of Giovanni Pico della Mirandola*, 1613-1621. Oil on canvas, 60 x 51 cm. Pinacoteca Ambrosiana, Milan. Photo Veneranda Biblioteca Ambrosiana/Mondadori Portfolio/akg-images

p. 136   Books on Charles Darwin's desk, Down House, Downe, Kent. Photo: Bridgeman Images

p. 138   Ruth Benedict, 1937. Library of Congress Prints and Photographs Division Washington, D.C.

p. 140   The first image of a black hole at the centre of the galaxy M87, taken by the Event Horizon Telescope, published 10 April 2019. Photo EHT

p. 142   Aksaray, province of Turkiye. Photo Yarr65/Alamy Stock Photo

p. 146   The Cha-no-yu, or Tea Ceremony, one of the Esoteric Arts of Japan, from Tetsudōin, *Sights and Scenes in Fair Japan* (Tokyo: Imperial Government Railways, c. 1910-1919)

p. 148   Trevi Fountain, Rome. Photo © Jundangoy/Dreamstime.com

p. 150   Le Corbusier, *Recherches sur les unités d'habitation*, façade sketch showing the brise-soleils, 1944. Black ink and pastel on tracing paper, 76.2 x 44.5 cm. Collection Fondation Le Corbusier (FLC 20566). © F.L.C./ADAGP, Paris and DACS, London 2023

p. 152   Brenda Prince, *Marion Milner*, 1997. © Brenda Prince, Format Photographers Archive @ Bishopsgate Institute, London

p. 154   Dick Bruna, *Miffy at the Zoo*, 1955. Published in the UK by Simon & Schuster (UK) Ltd. Illustration Dick Bruna © Mercis bv, 1963

p. 156   Kenneth Clark, *Civilisation* (London: BBC and John Murray, 1969)

p. 158   Elizabeth David, *An Omelette and a Glass of Wine* (London: Book Club Associates/ Dorling Kindersley, 1985); first published by Robert Hale/Jill Norman, 1984

p. 162   Engraving by Bernard Picart, *Villa Rotunda,* in Andrea Palladio, *The Architecture of A. Palladio in Four Books containing a Short Treatise on the Five Orders (L'Architecture de A. Palladio en quatre livres... / Il quattro libri dell'architettura)*, Volume 1, book 2, plate 15. Printed for the author by John Watts. Published London, 1715. Metropolitan Museum of Art, New York, Bequest of W. Gedney Beatty, 1941, Acc. 41.100.169(1.2.15)

p. 164   The Constitution of the United States of America, 1787. National Archives, Washington, D.C.

p. 166   René Magritte, *Les Vacances de Hegel (Hegel's Holidays)*, 1958. Oil on canvas, 59.5 x 50 cm. Private collection. Photo Luisa Ricciarini/Bridgeman Images © ADAGP, Paris and DACS, London 2023

p. 168   *Long Live the Thoughts of Chairman Mao*, propaganda poster from the Chinese Cultural Revolution, September 1969. Colour lithograph, 75 x 55 cm. Private Collection. Photo © The Chambers Gallery, London/Bridgeman Images

p. 170   Sophie Bassouls, *James Baldwin in Paris*, 1972. Photo Sophie Bassouls/Sygma via Getty Images

p. 172   Richard J. Novic, *Alice in Genderland* (London: iUniverse, 2005)

p. 176   Georg Melchior Kraus, *Soirée at the residence of Duchess Anna Amalia of Saxe-Weimar*, c. 1795. From left to right: H. Meyer, Frau von Fritsch, Goethe, Einsiedel, Anna Amalia, Elise Gore, Charles Gore, Frl. v. Göchhausen, Herder. Watercolour. Stiftung Weimarer Klassik, Weimar. Photo akg-images

p. 178   Gottlieb Schick, *Apollo Among the Shepherds*, 1806–1808. Oil on canvas, 178.5 × 232 cm. Staatsgalerie, Stuttgart. Photo: Erich Lessing/akg-images

p. 180   Gisèle Freund, *Virginia Woolf, London*, 1939. IMEC, Saint-Germain-la-Blanche-Herbe. Photo © 2023 RMN-Grand Palais /Dist. Photo SCALA, Florence © 2023 RMN gestion droit d'auteur/Fonds MCC/IMEC

p. 182   Crowds at the Paris Motor Show in the Grand Palais surround a Citroën DS-19 on display, October 1955. Photo Keystone/Hulton Archive/Getty Images

p. 184   Lucian Freud, *Sir Isaiah Berlin*, 1997. Graphite on paper, 38.1 x 28.6 cm. Private Collection. Photo © The Lucian Freud Archive. All Rights Reserved 2023/Bridgeman Images

p. 186   Marlis Schwieger, *Anaïs Nin*, 1950. Photo © Anais Nin Trust

p. 188   'I make the acquaintance of Miss Mowcher', illustration from Charles Dickens, *The Personal History of David Copperfield*, London: Chapman & Hall, 1900.

p. 192   Matthew Merian the Elder, *A Lion's Gratitude*, copper engraving from J.L. Gottfried, *Historische Chronica*, Frankfurt, 1630. Sammlung Archiv für Kunst und Geschichte, Berlin. Photo akg-images

p. 194   Torii Kiyonaga, *Murasaki Shikibu*, c. 1779–1789. Colour woodblock print, 36.1 x 24.5 cm. Art Institute of Chicago, Clarence Buckingham Collection, 1925.2642

p. 196   Suad al-Attar, *From a Thousand and One Nights 1*, 1984. Oil on canvas. Private Collection. Photo © Suad al-Attar. All Rights Reserved 2023/Bridgeman Images

p. 198   Illustration from Johann Wolfgang von Goethe, *Wilhelm Meister's Apprenticeship*, c. 1802. Engraving. Photo Bridgeman Images

p. 200   Cassandra Austen, *Portrait of Jane Austen*, c. 1810. Pencil and watercolour, 11.4 x 8 cm. National Portrait Gallery, London (NPG 3630). Photo © National Portrait Gallery, London

p. 202   Antoni Kozakiewicz, *Matthias, King of Kings* in *Pan Tadeusz*, Book VI, 1879. Oil on canvas, 44 x 55 cm. Muzeum Okręgowe w Lesznie, Leszno

p. 204   Illustration from Gustave Flaubert, *Madame Bovary*, first serialised in *La Revue de Paris*, 1 October-15 December 1856. Translated from the French, with critical introduction by Henry James, London: William Heinemann, 1902. Photo Lebrecht Authors/Bridgeman Images

p. 206   Marcel Proust kneeling and holding a tennis racket in front of Jeanne Ponquet (the Gilberte de Proust) at the tennis court of Boulevard Bineau in Neuilly, 1892. Photo © Doppio/Bridgeman Images

p. 208   Front Cover of *Il Gattopardo (The Leopard)* by Giuseppe Tomasi di Lampedusa, 1958. State Central Literary Museum, Moscow. Photo Fototeca Gilardi/Bridgeman Images

p. 210 Goscinny & Sempé, *Le petit Nicolas* (*Little Nicholas*) (London: Longman Group Ltd, 1967); first published by Denoël, Paris, 1960

p. 214   Dia al-Azzawi, *The Seven Golden Odes (The Mu'allaqat)*, 1978. Silkscreen print, 103 x 72 cm. © Dia Azzawi. All Rights Reserved, DACS 2023

p. 216   Yokoi Kinkoku, *The poet Basho with his most famous haiku, 'An old pond - a frog jumps in' from Haikai Gunsen No Zu (Portraits of Haiku Poets)*, c. 1820. British Library, London. Photo © British Library Board. All Rights Reserved/Bridgeman Images

p. 218   Scipio Moorhead, *Phillis Wheatley*, in Phillis Wheatley, *Poems on Various Subjects, Religious and Moral*, London: Archibald Bell, 1773. Collection of the Smithsonian National Museum of African American History and Culture, Washington, D.C., 2012.46.46

p. 220   Charles Pierre Baudelaire, *Jeanne Duval*, with an inscription to Paul Chenavard, c. 1862. Pen and ink on paper. Bibliothèque Litteraire Jacques Doucet, Paris. Photo © Archives Charmet/Bridgeman Images

p. 222   Augustus Leopold Egg, *Past and Present, No. 3*, 1858. Oil on canvas, 63.5 × 76.2 cm. Tate, London. Presented by Sir Alec and Lady Martin in memory of their daughter Nora, 1918. Photo: Tate, London

p. 224   Rabindranath Tagore, 1930s. Photo by Keystone-France/Gamma-Keystone via Getty Images

p. 226   Apkar Retian, *C.P. Cavafy*, undated. © 2016-2018 Cavafy Archive, Onassis Foundation

p. 228   Thomas Sturge Moore, front cover of W.B. Yeats, *The Tower,* 1928. Colour lithograph, 19.2 x 12.9 cm. Private collection. Photo © Christie's Images/Bridgeman Images

p. 230   W.H. Auden reading on the veranda, 1940s. Private Collection. Photo © James & Tania Stern Literary Estate. All Rights Reserved 2023/Bridgeman Images

p. 232   Paul M. Smith, *Joan Armatrading*, April 1983. Photo Pictorial Press Ltd/Alamy Stock Photo

p. 236   Raymond Auguste Quinsac Monvoisin, *Telemachus and Eucharis*, 1824. Oil on canvas, 294.6 x 251.5 cm. Minneapolis Institute of Art, Gift of Andrew A. Lynn (Acc. 78.25)

p. 238   Diary writing. Photo © Evgenyatamanenko/Dreamstime.com

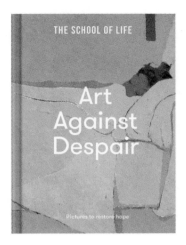

Art Against Despair
Pictures to restore hope

An inspiring selection of images offering us hope and comfort, reminding us that we are not alone in our sorrow.

One of the most unexpectedly useful things we can do when we're feeling glum or out of sorts is to look at pictures. The best works of art can lift our spirits, remind us of what we love and return perspective to our situation. A few moments in front of the right picture can rescue us.

This is a collection of the world's most consoling and uplifting images, accompanied by small essays that talk about the works in a way that offers us comfort and inspiration. The images in the book range wildly across time and space: from ancient to modern art, east to west, north to south, taking in photography, painting, abstract and figurative art. All the images have been carefully chosen to help us with a particular problem we might face: a broken heart, a difficulty at work, the meanness of others, the challenges of family and friends ...

We're invited to look at art with unusual depth and then find our way towards new hope and courage. This is a portable museum dedicated to beauty and consolation, a unique book about art which is also about psychology and healing: a true piece of art therapy.

ISBN: 978-1-912891-90-0

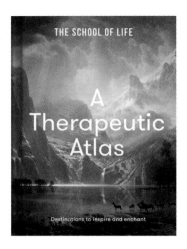

A Therapeutic Atlas
Destinations to inspire and enchant

A selection of unique and beautiful destinations around the world, which offer powerful new perspectives on life.

The world is full of places with an unusual power to inspire and bring us joy; they might be exceptionally beautiful, resonant with history, untouched by civilisation or rich in the right sort of memories.

This is an atlas that gathers together some of the most enchanting and reinvigorating places around the world in order to heal and captivate us. A perfect book for keen travellers, it takes us to beautiful destinations in Greece, Italy, Japan, America, Chile and Australia – to name but a few. We're taken to the tops of mountains, to solitary cliffs, elegant cities – and also to some less expected locations: airports, hydroelectric stations and meteorite craters.

Great travellers have always known that travelling can broaden the mind; here we see how it can also heal it. Tempting images are combined with short essays that discuss the power of particular places to help us with the difficulties of being human. We visit places that are 'therapeutic' because they coax us out of familiar patterns of thought and liberate our minds.

This is a book that can be read when we are travelling or when we are at home. It will remind us of the many places we still want to see – and more broadly, the many reasons we have to stay hopeful.

ISBN: 978-1-912891-93-1

A History of Ideas

The most intriguing, relevant and helpful concepts from
the story of humanity

A collection of humanity's most inspiring ideas throughout time, bringing perspective to the challenges and wonders of being alive.

This is an unusual history book: it is a history of ideas, and not just any old ideas, but the ones from across time and space that are best suited to healing, enchanting and reviving us. It is a collection of humanity's very best thoughts on how to approach the challenges and joys of being alive.

We travel around the world, from the very beginnings of our species right up to the modern age. We hear from the Ancient Greeks and Romans, we learn about Buddhism and Islam, we acquire ideas from Hinduism and the European Renaissance, the Enlightenment and Modernity. Deliberately eclectic, the book gives us a panoramic, 3,000-year view of the finest insights from a diversity of civilisations.

Every idea hangs off an image – a place, a document, a building or a work of art – that has something specific to teach us. There are ideas here that will stick in our minds because they can help to answer the biggest puzzles we may have: about the direction of our lives, the issues of relationships, and the meaning of existence.

The book is a feast for the intellect and the imagination with the intention to make us into the best sorts of historians: those of us who use the past to shed light on our own lives.

ISBN: 978-1-912891-96-2

Confidence in 40 Images

The art of self-belief

A curated selection of 40 photographs and artworks with accompanying essays examining the skill of confidence.

The difference between success and failure often comes down to an ingredient that we are seldom directly taught about and may forget to focus on: confidence.

What makes one life cheerful, purposeful and energetic and another less so may have nothing to do with intelligence or qualifications; it may simply be bound up with that buoyancy of the heart and mind we call confidence – the quality that gives us the courage to give things a go, to believe in ourselves and to resist the pull of conformity, fear and despair.

Here is a supreme guide to this fatefully neglected quality; a series of encouraging essays that jog us into a new and more fruitful state of mind. The images that accompany the text are there to ensure that we aren't merely intellectually stirred to change our lives, but that we are also given the best kind of visual assistance.

Although modest in size, this book succeeds at a mighty feat: unlocking our latent powers and edging us on with kindness and creativity to become the best version of ourselves.

ISBN: 978-1-915087-30-0

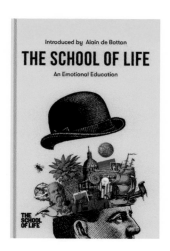

The School of Life:
An Emotional Education

How to live wisely and well in the twenty-first century – an introduction to the modern art of emotional intelligence.

Emotional intelligence affects every aspect of the way we live, from romantic to professional relationships, from our inner resilience to our social success. It is arguably the single most important skill for surviving the twenty-first century. But what does it really mean?

Fifteen years ago, Alain de Botton founded The School of Life, an institute dedicated to understanding and improving our emotional intelligence. Now he presents the gathered wisdom of those ten years in a wide-ranging and innovative compendium of emotional intelligence that forms an introduction to The School of Life. Using his trademark mixture of analysis and anecdote, philosophical insight and practical wisdom, he considers how we interact with each other and with ourselves, and how we can do so better. From the beloved expert of popular philosophy, *The School of Life: An Emotional Education* is an essential look at the skill set that defines our modern lives.

ISBN: 978-1-912891-45-0

The School of Life publishes a range of books on essential topics in psychological and emotional life, including relationships, parenting, friendship, careers and fulfilment. The aim is always to help us to understand ourselves better and thereby to grow calmer, less confused and more purposeful. Discover our full range of titles, including books for children, here:

www.theschooloflife.com/books

The School of Life also offers a comprehensive therapy service, which complements, and draws upon, our published works:

www.theschooloflife.com/therapy